GROWING OLD
DISGRACEFULLY

About the Authors

Mary Cooper was born in 1924. She was in the Women's Land Army from 1942 to 1945, married an RAF man and had four daughters. She took a degree at the age of 41, and was divorced in 1980. Mary has worked in adult education, mainly women's education, and has always wanted to write the book that would change the world.

Shirley Meredeen, a procrastinator all her life, intends to carry on as usual by putting death off as long as possible. Meantime, she has enjoyed her life as a mature student and provincial journalist, and continues to do so as a senior citizen, divorcee, mother-in-law, grandmother, freelance counsellor, trainer and conciliator. She was born in 1930 in London to immigrant parents.

Edith Redstone was born in New York in 1918. She survived the Great Depression of the 1930s with a variety of jobs and a BA degree. She married in 1942 and arrived in England in 1944. Another series of occupations followed as well as two children and six grandchildren. She lives in London and is a part-time director of an art gallery.

Barbara Tayler was born in London in 1931, married at 20 while at London University and after graduating spent the next eight years nurturing her first three children. She started work with an educational trust, left to have her fourth child, then returned to the trust eventually becoming the Director. Now she is revelling in retirement and in growing old disgracefully.

Maxine Myers is a Texan by birth, a Californian by choice. Schooled until age 14, she has been getting educated ever since. She spent 17 years working inside the home as wife, mother and community activist, returning to formal education at age 42. She completed a Doctorate in Sociology at 54, and is currently the Director of a College Women's Centre and a lecturer in Women's Studies.

Anne Woolf was born in London in 1930, married in 1955, and has a son and a daughter. She feels her most creative education was received at evening classes. She did voluntary work before qualifying as a social worker in 1976. Now divorced and happily retired, she enjoys dance and art classes, bird-watching, walking, swimming and wearing purple.

GROWING OLD
DISGRACEFULLY

New ideas for getting the most out of life

THE HEN CO-OP

PIATKUS

First published in 1993 by
Judy Piatkus (Publishers) Ltd
5 Windmill Street, London W1P 1HF

Reprinted 1993

The moral right of the authors has been asserted

*A catalogue record for this book is available
from the British Library*

ISBN 0-7499-1219-7
ISBN 0-7499-1261-8 (Pbk)

Designed by Zena Flax
Illustrations by Angela Martin
Cover photograph by Vaughan Melzer
Photographs of authors in Chapter One
   all by Vaughan Melzer, apart from the
   photograph of Mary Cooper which was taken
   by Shirley Meredeen

Typeset by Action Typesetting Ltd, Gloucester
Printed and bound in Great Britain by
Butler and Tanner Ltd, Frome

Contents

Introduction

A year or so before she retired, Mary Cooper had the idea of putting on a special course for older people. It was part of her job to devise and teach innovatory adult education courses. She did not want the course to be about retirement or even pre-retirement; she wanted it to be something totally new, to inspire women to challenge the accepted views of growing old in a dynamic way.

It was about the same time that she heard of a course for older women at the Hen House, a holiday and study centre for women only, in Lincolnshire. The first such course, under the intriguing name of 'Growing Old Disgracefully', was highly successful and soon the Hen House was holding many Growing Old Disgracefully courses for which Mary became the regular facilitator. The courses have a powerful impact on the women who attend, and women who have taken part in the courses have begun to organise local networks (see page 224 for details). One such group was formed by us, the six members of the Hen Co-op, who all met on the July 1989 course. Mary herself is one of us.

'We *must* write a book about growing old disgracefully,' we all said, and so we kept meeting, talking and listening to each other, writing, rewriting and collecting materials. We made false starts, discarded writings that we had put a lot of work into and wondered if indeed we would ever accomplish what we had set out to do. Here we were, six women all past the age of 60, none of us professional writers, and we were presuming to know how to pull this off. Although some of us had been published before, none of us had ever tried group authorship, nor did we have any models to follow. We found the task daunting at times but invariably joyful. After all, there is something disgraceful in itself about six ageing women getting together to do something that they have never done before.

We wanted our book to be different from what has already been written, so we searched bookstores and libraries to see what was available. Much of what we found was written by so-called experts, many of them males, who had studied women from a detached, once-removed clinical perspective, addressing mainly the physiological and pathological aspects of ageing.

There were books documenting ageism in social institutions and they were so thorough that we figured we did not need to focus in that direction, although we know first hand how important a topic this is. We hope that you will read some of those books and combat ageism where you find it (see Further Reading, page 219).

Other books were about 'exceptional' women: the rich and famous celebrities who were glorified for 'not looking their age', another form of ageism. Then there were the 'I-climbed-Mt-Everest-on-my-83rd-birthday' types. Inspiring, yes, but spotlighted for the very reason that they are out of the ordinary. What was missing were the voices of women like ourselves. Even the British feminist authors who have greatly enriched our understanding of women on so many levels have had very little to say about ageing women.

We decided that since there are plenty of people much more knowledgeable and qualified to address the physical and biological aspects of ageing, we would leave to them the task of explaining how to treat osteoporosis and the pros and cons of hormone replacement therapy. Nor did we want this to be a book on diet and exercise. We will just start from the assumption that there is enough conflicting evidence on nutrition and physical activity to have driven you to sensible moderation by now.

A how-to manual? No – we figured that growing old disgracefully means getting rid of the shoulds and oughts that have been running women's lives for so long, and besides, who were we to tell you what to do? In the end, we decided that what we had to offer was to speak in our own voices about our own experiences and maybe some of you would find us speaking to your experiences as well. We recognise our privileges as white middle-class women and do not presume that our circumstances are representative of all women, or that what works for us would necessarily be appropriate for everyone. We hope, though, that you enjoy reading our book as much as we enjoyed the process of writing it.

Through our collaboration over the past few years we have learned much about group process and compromise. We developed our own style of working together which usually consisted of discussing a subject then going off individually to write about it, after which we would get back together to discuss what each of us had written. After comments and suggestions, there would be revisions or re-writes and again the group would comment. The intro-ductions to each chapter were written by one person pulling together the concepts from everyone's writings and the discussions. It may have been unorthodox, but it worked for us. At the start and end of each session, we would play games, dance, sing, stretch and loosen up. We would almost always repeat some of this when we felt we were getting tired and stale.

We were new friends so we had to take time in the beginning to identify what we had in common and how we differed. This invariably brought out past histories, including previously unexplored delights and pains. Writing sometimes had to stop while we helped each other work through feelings that were paramount at the moment.

When we were writing, we often stayed together for days

at a time, sharing food, chores and living space. A few times we clubbed together to rent or borrow cottages away from the distractions of our everyday lives so that we could spend the time concentrating on the writing. We alternated hosting, cooking and washing-up, never having to assign tasks or remind each other.

After all the togetherness, you might wonder if we are still on speaking terms with one another, but we can only assure you that the intensity of these times cemented our friendships. The physical and emotional closeness restimulated memories of the warm comfort of a family group and, for some of us, the lack of that experience. We came to realise how terribly important it is for women our age to form new primary friendship groups, distinct from the roles we have played in the past.

Besides our friendships, one of the best things to come out of our collaboration has been our rediscovery of laughter. Women have always been familiar with tears but when six women find so much to laugh about together, we know that we have already crossed the line into growing old disgracefully. And when tears came, as inevitably they did, we felt them diffuse through the group and somehow the burden lightened. We heartily recommend both the laughter and the tears.

We offer you this book as a collage of past, present and future, overlapping one another and forming an impression more than a representation. To begin, we introduce ourselves through short life stories, then fill in some of the background that led us to our present state of growing old disgracefully, which we go on to define and illustrate in Chapter 4. The chapter on sex and sensuality reflects our own struggles to come to terms with our bodies and to place them in the context of sexuality as we age. Finally, we project into a possible future which would include a disgraceful very old age. Our last words in Chapter 7 will bring you up-to-date on what is happening with us now and how we have been affected by writing this book.

We are grateful to Rachel Lever for providing the Growing Old Disgracefully courses at her women-only holiday and learning centre, the Hen House. References to the Hen House and the course appear throughout the book and as you read them you will come to know why we so readily express our gratitude.

Above all, we thank Judy Piatkus, Gill Cormode and Heather Rocklin of Piatkus Books for their constructive help and for trusting that six old women who had a crazy idea that they could write a book would actually do it.

Maxine lives in California but managed to spend six months with us to work on this book. The rest of us would like to express our thanks for her special contribution in writing the introductions to the chapters.

CHAPTER ONE

Telling
Our Stories

When we first got the idea for this book, we agreed it should begin with some background about ourselves, to see if we could find the events and turning points that led us to this stage of growing old disgracefully. We had no idea how empowering the telling of our stories would become.

Before we could begin, we went through the gamut of disclaimers about our own participation:

'I can't write well enough.'

'I have nothing important to say.'

'My life is not unusual – who'd want to read about it?'

It is true that we had all lived more or less ordinary lives in the ways that women do, or thought we had, anyway. But here we were, six women from varying backgrounds, all having made it through wars, financial ups and downs, jobs, marriages, births, deaths, divorces, disillusionments, successes, and all the public and private events of more than 60 years running, and we were claiming to have nothing of interest to say!

Women in general, and old women in particular, have had our voices silenced or distorted in so many ways that it is sometimes difficult to think of words that express what is important to us. When we finally start to say them aloud, we release ourselves from the restrictions that have been put on us by others. We are affirming that our lives are important.

The six of us had great fun sharing our stories with each other. We found that when we finally found our own voices, comparing our experiences became the bedrock of our friendship. On that foundation, we were able to build up trust, and go on to more risky subjects, as you will find in later chapters.

Looking at the past is not as easy as it seems. Memory can be selective, as Barbara found:

> When I look at the past, I see a series of disconnected images, in no particular order. Sometimes details stand out with great clarity, but their background is blurred. Often the details that come into sharpest focus seem inconsequential, even trivial. But their secure place in memory implies that they are not trivial at all.

It may not be important to be entirely factual when telling your story. The disgracefulness comes from talking about yourself. We found that it was not what we said or how we said it that made the difference in feeling better about ourselves. It was the process of speaking and being listened to that was empowering. As we recounted things we had done in our lives, we began to appreciate that even though we had followed ordinary patterns, we had accomplished more than we had given ourselves credit for.

Every woman has a story to tell. We encourage you to tell yours. When you re-examine your life, you will begin to see influences that will help you understand who you are today. Ideally, gather a group of women of your own generation and share your stories with each other. If that's not possible, write your story down and add to it when you think of something more.

Each person's story is unique, each is full of fascination in its own way; however, if you take them together, you will begin to find themes and patterns. First, notice how the qualities of resilience and strength come through in your own and in other women's stories. See how courage, perseverance, energy and determination move the stories along.

Look for the turning points, try to identify when each woman, facing her own old age, realises there has to be more to look forward to than conventional patterns of ageing. To grow old disgracefully means to find ways to break these established patterns and seize the opportunity to choose your own direction.

The following life stories illustrate what we mean. Each of us turned our lives around by taking risks, long before any of us recognised or put words to the concept of growing old disgracefully. For example, Shirley returned at 52 to get her Open University degree after years of interruptions; Anne left home and husband when she was 50; Edith is staying at her part-time job in spite of criticism from friends that she isn't attending to her husband's needs. How these changes take shape may be different for each of us, but in some way, each is saying 'I have a self, and I will find my own path to nurturing that self.'

Lack of space meant we had to leave out details that might have enriched our autobiographies. We were forced to make difficult choices about what to include and what to leave out. The more we wrote, the more we recalled people and events, until each of our stories alone could have filled a book. We hope that you will get to know each of us as you read this and subsequent chapters. We also hope that by reading our stories you will be inspired to tell your own . . .

ANNE

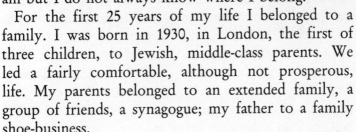

For many years of my life I was not sure who I was but I knew where I belonged. Over the last few years I have gradually come to know who I am but I do not always know where I belong.

For the first 25 years of my life I belonged to a family. I was born in 1930, in London, the first of three children, to Jewish, middle-class parents. We led a fairly comfortable, although not prosperous, life. My parents belonged to an extended family, a group of friends, a synagogue; my father to a family shoe-business.

In 1939, when I was nine, war broke out and the family moved 30 miles out of London, into the countryside, where I spent my early adolescence. I did moderately well at the local grammar school, became a patrol-leader in the Girl Guides, enjoyed the freedom of the countryside on my bicycle, with my friends. My best friend from the age of nine was Judith, who came over to England from Germany in 1939 with the Kinder-transport (a scheme to bring children out of Nazi Germany), to live nearby with a family who were friends of my parents. We did everything together – I loved her dearly, with two exceptions – all the boys I liked, liked her better than me and she always beat me on sports day at long-distance throwing. Despite that, over 50 years later we are still friends.

I now belonged to a family, a peer group at school, a youth club, and a circle of friends, mostly from that club. Although I was shy I enjoyed playing Postman's Knock and Truth or Dare, climbing trees on the common and riding my bicycle.

At the end of the war, when I was 15, we returned to London. I started at a new school – in the sixth form, as I had now matriculated. It was a difficult time to start meeting and making new friends. I joined a tennis club where I played quite a good game and I became a member of a youth club, but my school-work was affected by the move and I left after spending two years in the lower sixth.

What to do next? I struggled with various ideas but do not feel I had much guidance. I was not very competitive, not very sure of myself. I was accepted at an art school but, as there were no immediate vacancies, my thoughts of becoming a stage designer evaporated. Different ideas came and went – should I be a librarian? A radiographer? After a few days my enthusiasm for each of these ideas disappeared and I ended up on a secretarial course, with French and book-keeping. For six months I belonged to a group of rather upper-class 'gels' doing an intensive secretarial course. Afterwards, with my new skills I applied for, and got, a job as a secretary.

It seems strange to me now but I don't remember belonging to any political party or supporting any cause. Somehow, these ideas did not come my way at that time of my life.

I went to parties and I had boy-friends, but my shyness and passivity dogged me and, if I could get out of accepting invitations, I did. I preferred to stay at home and read. After one party, when I was 19, I was taken home by a good-looking law student who was the same age as me. We began to go out together frequently and after two years we became engaged. Then, because he had to finish his studies and do National Service, it was another four years before we got married, just after our 25th birthdays.

So started the second 25-year period of my life. I now belonged to a husband and his family as well as my own – he then had three elderly grandparents living (I had none), his parents, and many uncles, aunts and cousins. We had two children: a son and then a daughter – just what I had hoped for. We lived just outside London, in a new house, and I was happy. I belonged to a set of young mothers with children. We had tea-parties together, swam with our children, played tennis and went to Scottish country-dancing classes in the evening when the husbands came home to babysit. We exchanged childcare with each other, as we all lived near one another in similar new houses. I somehow imagined that I would be going to tea-parties and visiting friends for the rest of my life.

But, of course, the children started school and then there was time to reconsider – what did I want to do now? I knew that being a housewife was not enough for me. I went to various evening classes – literature, music, art appreciation – and received an education and love of those subjects which was never properly fostered at school. I started doing voluntary work with the local Probation Service, then with the Citizens' Advice Bureau. I became Honorary Organiser of a newly-formed CAB and was lucky enough to represent the organisation at a Royal Garden Party. I joined the Liberal party and was asked to stand for the local parish and town councils. I became a well-known citizen in my area and my views were often quoted in the papers. I decided to start training for a career in social work and, after five years' part-time study, I obtained a Diploma in Social Studies. I then worked part-time as a medical social-worker in a local hospital, strutting around, feeling important, in a starched white coat, carrying a bleeper! Two years later, I was a student again on a professional course at London University. With my Certificate of Qualification in Social Work I was ready for full-time work with a London Borough. It was exciting, stimulating, and I received a good salary.

I was changing, expanding, but I was beginning to feel that my marriage did not provide the nurturing and stimulation I needed. My husband and I were both bad communicators and so nothing was ever resolved.

During our married life we belonged to a large group of couples, many professional and with children of similar ages to our own. We entertained each other at dinner parties where we discussed cars, holidays and our children's achievements, and we went to the cinema and theatre together.

The children became teenagers with lives of their own and I began to feel there must be more to life. The dinner parties began to pall, communication with my husband continued to deteriorate. Who was I? – a wife, a mother – but who was I?

The turning point in my life came just before my 50th birthday and our 25th wedding anniversary. How could I celebrate a silver wedding when the marriage now felt devoid of the love, affection, companionship and respect that we once had? I knew there could be more to life. Either I had to act now or resolve to make the best of the remaining years of my life in my marriage.

I decided against the celebration. My husband said nothing when I told him I was going to leave and he made no attempt to stop me. At the end of 1981 we were divorced and, shortly after that, he remarried. We are still on good terms and I enjoy seeing him and his wife from time to time.

It was the right decision for me – I could not find my true 'self' within the marriage and it was a great relief to be on my own. I often saw my children but my work colleagues became my family base, my network – they were very caring and supportive, as were my sister and my friends.

Twenty-five years single, 25 years married – now for the future, which I faced with excitement and apprehension. Where did I belong now? I joined a massage group and two women's consciousness-raising groups. My first flat was a very special place – my nest, and

all my own. My personal development really started at
this point – the world was my oyster. I was free.

I had always valued my women friends; now they
became all-important to me. I was amazed at the topics
we discussed frankly in the consciousness-raising groups
– pornography, assertiveness, harassment, relationships, alternative ways of living, sexist language,
separatism, lesbianism. Women sharing the joy and
pain in their lives with honesty brought us all close
together. My head was spinning from so many ideas
and concepts.

I went with women to Greenham Common and
experienced the solidarity of women determined to
make the world a safer, more peaceful place to live. I
sewed part of a banner, to be connected to hundreds of
other banners for peace from all over the world, for the
Dragon Festival. We stayed there at full moon, singing,
chanting, surrounding ourselves in a mesh of wool, an
unbroken web, cutting fences, protesting for peace –
'take the toys from the boys!'

And I fell in love with a woman. We went to a
massage group and we shared massage at home. I felt
soft and loved and cared for under her gentle hands.
Our ensuing relationship was short-lived but I would
not have missed that brief intimacy. My feelings were
so chaotic that I started individual therapy which
helped me learn to recognise and accept parts of myself
which I had not known even existed.

So many endings, so many beginnings. I wanted an
intimate relationship, and I wanted this relationship to
be with a woman. I met that women the first time I
went to a meeting of the Older Lesbian Network and
we became lovers and loving companions. We travelled
together and enjoyed many wonderful holidays. After
about two years we agreed to buy a flat together
although, with hindsight, neither of us believed it
would work out. It didn't! We lived in the flat for eight

months before we sold it and I moved again, to live on my own in my present flat. I learned how important it is for me to have lots of space, both geographical and emotional, and the idea of living with someone again stifles and threatens me.

I have started on the path to knowing who I am but there is still the question, where do I belong?

It was about a year after the end of my relationship and coming up to the age of retirement that I signed up for the course 'Growing Old Disgracefully' at the Hen House.

Anne

BARBARA

How do you condense 60 years of life into so few pages without losing the essence, the quality which makes each life unique? Once you begin to write, so many memories flood in, each demanding a place. But we have had to be ruthless, limiting ourselves to the bare bones. So, here goes.

Part 1: My Mother's Daughter

I am told that I was a bright, pretty, clever child with curly hair – a little Shirley Temple. My mother was very proud of me, she often told me so. She came from a very close Jewish family of seven sisters and three brothers, most of whom lived within a few streets of each other in Stamford Hill. I have no memories of my father who died when I was two. My mother and I lived with one or other of her sisters until the war started, then, during the war, my mother and I and her only unmarried sister lived in furnished 'digs' in Swansea. So my whole childhood was spent in other people's houses.

Like many single women my mother and aunt had a great social life during the war and by the time I was about 11 or 12 they were out most nights. I was not alone in the house but I was *alone*. I would do my homework, then read unsuitable books such as *Forever Amber* or listen to *Appointment with Fear* or other such unsuitable programmes on the wireless and put myself to bed.

When the war ended we moved back to London and for the first time we had our own home, a dark basement flat in Maida Vale. I had my own room where daylight never penetrated but I thought it was wonderful. My mother and aunt continued to share not only a room but a double bed. They were inseparable yet they argued all the time: they bickered about everything from the size of the sugar-lumps in the bowl to the brightness of the light-bulbs. But memory can be so selective. I know it would be wrong to remember only the solitary child – but there were good times too. Yet if I shut my eyes and try to visualise an image labelled 'Childhood' I see myself outside a window, looking in at a jolly family in a cheerful, brightly-lit, warm room. The sadness and envy of this image still gives me pain.

Part 2: My Husband's Wife

Just before Christmas 1950, in my second year at university, I met the man who became my husband. It disturbs me to look back at that hopeful 19-year-old child who knew at the first meeting that this was the man with whom she wanted to share her life. How could she have been so sure? He was an architect, ten years older than me, a mature ex-serviceman. When he asked me to marry him I agreed with no hesitation, despite the fact that he was not Jewish. Overcoming family objections, we had a small registry office wedding and I went back to my final year of university as a respectable married lady.

We found a flat in the house of some friends and while I studied for my Finals, Julian worked on his thesis to complete a course as a planner. We played at house together, worked hard, laughed a lot and learned to live with each other. On the day after my last exam we set off for a holiday in France with a tent and all our belongings strapped to the back of a motor-bike. We arrived home to two pieces of news: I had got an Upper Second and I was pregnant.

I was 22 when our first son, Steve, was born and I was overwhelmed by the joy of being a mother. I loved the sensual pleasure of holding this sweet milky little being. I loved breast-feeding, I loved all the paraphernalia of babies but above all I loved the feeling that we were a family unit, that I was now inside the window. Since Julian and I had both grown up without fathers we had no role models to accept or reject. We had to re-invent the role of father for ourselves, we had to feel our way into the new dynamic of our family with no map to guide us. But, on the whole, we felt that we were doing quite well, we enjoyed our marriage and loved being parents.

Over the next few years we moved from town to town as Julian rose up the promotion ladder and our next two children were born: another boy, Simon, then a daughter, Kath. My days became totally child-orientated. Steve started school and had to be taken and fetched morning, lunchtime and afternoon. Four times a day I would load the other two into the pram and rush the mile or so to school and back again. Julian had to leave for work at 8.00 and did not get home until about 6.30. Looking back I see how much he missed of the children's lives while, despite the hard work, I found this time very fulfilling. I had made friends in our new neighbourhood and I was involved in the peace movement. At the time of the first Aldermaston March in 1958, I was eight months pregnant, so I did not march but I was part of the first CND group in our area.

I was very happy. I did not feel oppressed or deprived or dissatisfied. I felt myself to be the hub of our little family and organising the running of the house was the background to the joy of watching the children grow and develop. I felt that I was a real mum in a way that my mother had never been. I cuddled them and told them how much I loved them and as I kissed their tender necks I would be overcome by the realisation that I could not remember my mother ever kissing me and telling me that she loved me.

In 1960 there were two important changes which marked turning points for our marriage. Julian took up acting with a local amateur theatre and I was offered a part-time job with an educational publisher. They do not sound significant or monumental changes but his involvement with the theatre marked the beginning of the end of the best part of our marriage, while my part-time job grew into a stimulating and fulfilling career which lasted for the rest of my working life. Things did not seem to change so drastically at the time, it was just that our interests began to develop along separate paths and outside the family. We both felt that this was a healthy development at that stage in our lives. And while he was busy with the theatre I was active in CND and belonged to the local Housebound Housewives, which later became the Housewives' Register. For me this period was crucial in establishing friendship networks with other women – friendships which were to sustain me through the bad times which were to come – while Julian's involvement at the theatre, where he was mixing with many younger people at a less encumbered stage in their lives, had the effect of making him feel restless and constricted.

When our fourth child, Ben, was born I gave up work – there was no maternity leave then – and once more I relished the time spent at home. Perhaps I chose not to see that Julian was less than thrilled by the restrictions on our lives caused by having another baby. He was busy with the theatre and I became more and more involved in peace activities as the full horror of the Vietnam war was revealed.

A group of us in Ealing formed a local committee for Medical Aid for Vietnam, our ambitions were unlimited and everything we undertook grew beyond our dreams. Our lives as a group became intertwined. And then some of our lives became too intertwined – we later referred to this period as a collective madness. We did not realise that we were all conforming to the pattern of the Swinging Sixties. In 1970, when Ben was three, I discovered that Julian had been having an affair for the previous six months with my closest friend in the group. All the certainties disappeared. The glass smashed, the inside vanished and I felt that I was on the outside of the window again.

For two years we carried on living together one way or another and life went on. In 1971, in the midst of all this family crisis, two good things happened in the same week. I was offered my old job part-time and, as a result of my Vietnam activity, I was invited to go to Cuba to a celebration of International Women's Day. I celebrated my fortieth birthday in Havana surrounded by strong loving women from all parts of the world. There had to be more to life than one man who had decided that he no longer loved me. I went back to work with more confidence and optimism after this visit and the work became more and more fascinating as I took on more responsibility. The company had been formed into a non-profit-making Trust, the ethos was one with which I could totally identify and the work was stimulating and mind-stretching. But at home, seeing myself through Julian's eyes was destroying my self-esteem, he made me feel not just unloved but unlovable. So when, in May 1972, he decided to leave I did not try to stop him. I was left alone with three teenagers and a five-year-old about to start school.

Part 3: My Children's Mother

But it was so hard. Running a home and a job, dealing with teenage traumas and five-year-old tantrums and going to bed lonely. My greatest source of strength was the network of women friends, sustaining, not judging, sharing, laughing and crying together. Four of us became particular friends and began to meet regularly to help each other through the bad times and to share the good times too. We always had time for each other and still have, over 20 years later.

I stayed in the family home and let some rooms to lodgers as one by one the older children left, then came back, then left again. I bitterly resented the destruction of my image of the happy 'inside' family. I felt impotent in controlling the path of my life. I did not want to live alone. I had not chosen to bring up children alone. I could not admit to any share in the responsibility for the breakdown of our marriage. But during these years I somehow held the family together, developed my job, cared for and visited the three old ladies – my mother, aunt and mother-in-law – who all depended on me for support, continued my political involvement and tried to make our home a good place to be. I suffered continual and serious ill-health which necessitated many stays in hospital. Life was not a bed of roses.

In 1980, with only one child still at home, I moved to a smaller house which I was able to buy outright. We did the move ourselves in a borrowed van, my sons and their friends ferrying load after load while I supervised and made endless cups of tea. It felt good to have my own place with no associations with our married life – I wondered why I had not made a move sooner. In the following year I was promoted to Director at work and the sad 1970s began to recede. I began to feel that I was creating my own 'inside the window' for Ben and myself – a warm, light place where we were happy. But Ben was growing up, needing his own space and his own life, separate from mine. Once again I was going to have to face loss and the prospect frightened me. I did not know how I was going to face life without a child to nurture after so many years of mothering. I decided to prepare myself by going into therapy well before the time came.

Therapy is not an easy path to choose, the process is painful. But gradually I began to make contact with the child within, to love and understand that child and give her permission to assert her rights. This was my first major step towards growing old disgracefully. At last I began to understand that I had only ever allowed myself time off from responsibilities when I was ill and that there might be a connection between my ill-health and my need to be nurtured. In January 1988 I ended therapy feeling more confident and positive about the future. Although the needs of the aged parents were still great, I felt more able to draw clear boundaries without feeling guilty about the things I could not do for them. Then in 1989 Ben moved out. It was the end of my 36 years as a mother-hen.

Part 4: Myself

Living alone for the first time in my life was a strange experience. I could not get used to shopping for one and kept having to throw food away because I had over-stocked. At first I found it hard to come home to an empty house but surprisingly soon it began to feel quite luxurious: I could choose whether to cook or not; the house stayed so much tidier with only me in it; there was more time to read or listen to music or do the crossword, or to spend with friends. My work was full of interest and stimulation and brought me into contact with a wide range of people. My life was pretty good. But one problem I found, as a single woman, was the overwhelming prevalence of 'couple-dom'. Nearly all my friends were still in couples and their lives with their partners took precedence over their lives as friends. And as my 60th birthday approached and retirement loomed I knew that I had to find a way to change my life. It was this need to find something more that led me to the Hen House in July 1989.

Barbara

EDITH

When I came to England in 1944 as a reverse war bride (my husband being English and I American) I was already 26 and had evolved as a person in my own right with an American past and an unknown British future. All my previous experience and education had been in the States, primarily New York. I had lived through some painfully difficult periods, having been born at the end of the First World War and grown up during a world-wide depression. There were undoubtedly bright periods, especially during the early years, but memories of the later ones were overshadowed by my family's struggle for survival, the doom-laden 1930s with the rise of anti-semitism in Nazi Germany and the cries for help from our relatives caught up in it.

Much of my development in the 1920s and particularly the 1930s was shaped by events over which I had no control, although I am sure I wasn't aware of it at the time. So when my father's small business collapsed, the Depression having finally caught up with us in the early 1930s, I was unprepared for the major changes in family life as I had known it. The ambitions and hopes of my immigrant parents were abandoned; the atmosphere of our previously pleasant home became sad and embittered as my mother undertook the main support of our household during my father's extended unemployment. It left him feeling useless, his confidence and general well-being slowly deteriorating. He would spend long hours just sitting by the window gazing into nothingness. In retrospect, I feel guilty that we as a family were not really supportive, blaming him for the hard times which had befallen us. That struggle for survival affected us all, leaving scars which never properly healed: I greatly resented first having to withdraw from college, but had no choice, and then having to search for a job and contribute my share towards household expenses. I did resume my studies at night, but working five and a half days a week, attending classes four nights, *and* keeping up my political involvement left very little time for anything else. I was determined to complete my studies and to also remain politically active in the American Student

Union, a politicised national student organisation I had joined on entering college. I was 18 at the start of this new regime, and it was to be another five years before I finally received my degree.

As events in Europe became more threatening and the Depression around us deepened, I found myself increasingly committed to 'Saving the World'. I was on an idealistic high in the company of many other young people, convinced that radical changes in attitudes were possible and that my efforts would help to effect this; fascism would be halted, and the United States economy would recover, resulting in a fairer distribution of wealth. I was certain I knew all the answers to the problems worldwide. My naïve dream ended quite suddenly with the signing of the Soviet-German Non-Aggression Pact in 1939. With hindsight I can now see that my reaction was precipitous and made without any real understanding of the situation. In a mood of disillusionment and disappointment I resigned from the Young Communist League of which by then I was a member, and never again affiliated with any political organisation except for a short spell in CND in the early 1960s.

In 1942 I married an Englishman I had met two years before and changed my job to one in a defence industry when the United States entered the war after the Japanese attack on Pearl Harbour. I was finally to utilise some of the education I had struggled so long and hard to complete. Scientific subjects, my specialisation in college, were dusted off and put to good use in my work as a quality control engineer overseeing the production of the electronic tubes for use in radar systems. It was a happy change from my previous clerical job and I felt satisfied and stimulated by the work, but when in 1944 my husband had to return to England, I was determined to accompany him. Overriding my parents' objections, I applied for and obtained a British passport after the U.S. State Department refused to issue an American one on the grounds that Great Britain was still considered a dangerous war zone. We left New York in October of that year with 400 other passengers on a New Zealand cargo ship called the *Rangitiki*. After picking up our convoy several hours later, we were on our way to England.

England in 1944 was a very different world from the one I had left behind. It wasn't just the war, although that was undoubtedly part of the problem. Despite the massive physical destruction nothing had really changed. Theoretically the war was supposed to have penetrated the barriers of class, education and sex; in practice, they were all still in place, especially where women were concerned (women were always in the ranks, almost never in the upper echelons). My own brief experience working in an American War Agency was different since everyone from the top echelons down was on first name terms, making for an informal atmosphere. Members of staff were frequently involved in decisions concerning the department and although physical conditions in the offices were positively primitive, for me it was 'Home from Home'.

Once away from the office things were radically different. I had difficulty coping with the formality of social occasions, unable to make contact except on a superficial level and my relationship with my husband's family was unsatisfactory as they did not really approve of working wives. My job with the US Office of Information helped to bridge the gap between the two worlds. It had been a fortunate coincidence that my search for essential war work (as an able-bodied British subject) coincided with a vacancy at the US Office of War Information. Fortunately this was considered acceptable employment by the authorities.

Although I had been in England for less than a year when the war ended in August 1945, I felt the need to return to the States before making my mind up whether to settle permanently in England. My job with the OWI was ending and all my American colleagues were leaving. I was feeling homesick for friends and family and for the easy social atmosphere of my home town. I was unsure of my future.

I remained in New York for three months, seeing people, looking after my very young niece while her mother (my sister) spent time alone with her wounded husband newly returned from the war in Europe. I was enjoying myself, but also having a long hard think, making certain in my own mind that I was prepared to give up New York and all that it meant to me, for England and uncertainty. Just before Christmas 1945 I made my decision, sailed for England and have been here ever since.

I sometimes feel I have been two different people and my long residence in Britain has reinforced that feeling. When I reflect on my life in the US and remember how politically aware and active I was then, how much more sensitive I was to what was happening around me, I find it hard to understand how politically uninvolved I have become during my stay in England, never motivated to act on any of the just causes that would have attracted me in my American period. When I listen to my five co-writers speaking about the Women's Movement and its influence on their lives, I wonder how it could have passed me by; it's almost as though I had been living in another world. Political disillusionment in the past could not solely account for it. Was it because I was so completely absorbed adjusting to a new pattern of living, seduced by a comfortable existence in the happy secure relationship that was missing during my youth, freed from monetary stress for the first time in my adult life? Part of the answer must surely be the strong support I received from my husband for everything I tackled. It was also the complete freedom of movement that was inherent in that support, enabling me to travel when my job required it, to visit family and friends in New York occasionally and even to go on holiday without him. Since I achieved the two I's, Independence and Identity, which have underpinned my life here within the confines of our own personal environment, I suppose I did not look elsewhere.

I had slipped easily into the new, cosy patterns that marriage and a family brought: taking pleasure in watching our two children develop in the early years; enjoying the space that our suburban house and garden provided; learning to grow my own fruit and vegetables. It presented such a different picture from anything I had experienced growing up in a crowded New York apartment and I enjoyed the luxury of it for a while, even though I knew that the time would come when just looking after the home would not provide me with complete satisfaction. Although basically I wasn't interested in a career, I did need the external stimulation and my own identity. Over the years I have engaged in a variety of occupations that have fulfilled those needs, both in the voluntary sector and in paid commercial work.

My present occupation as a director in a commercial art gallery commenced ten years ago. It is now very much on a part-time basis, but at that time my husband was still working and I was able to devote myself to this new, stimulating occupation. Things began to change when he retired six years ago, slowly at first, then radically. There was no longer a structure to his day and no new friends to replace the business colleagues who gradually drifted away. In addition, the bad effects of his old major chest operation 40 years previously were presenting problems, which included a low energy level. In consequence he spent a good deal of time either reading or resting, with my presence increasingly required. I was beginning to feel hemmed in as well as guilty if I was away from home for any long period during the day. It was at this point that I heard about the Hen House and arranged to take the 'Growing Old Disgracefully' course.

Edith

MARY

I left home in 1942 when I was 19 to join the Women's Land Army. I was longing to get away from my mother and what seemed her high-handed disapproving ways. The war made it easier – before then girls I knew only left home to marry or go into 'service' and only rarely to go to college or university. In the WLA I lived on a farm with the family and did all the jobs that needed doing. It was a rough little place on the edge of the Black Mountains, beautiful and remote, and I loved it.

My mother and father were divorced when my twin sister and I were eight. I had no happy memories of my father, only painful and disturbing ones. We had no grandfathers, uncles, boy cousins or brothers. We went to the local girls' grammar school where all the teachers were single women – dedicated teachers they were, but their singleness made them seem unenviable as women.

To fill up the gaps in my life I invented a companion and lover, an idealised, male version of myself whose name was David. A mixture of Shelley and Beethoven with the looks of Rupert Brooke; an intellectual whose understanding of women (me in particular) was the greater part of his nature; as capable of manual work as of writing poetry or playing the violin; at home in town or country, ordering a meal in a posh hotel or dancing under the trees in the moonlight. However did I get so caught up with such absurd notions of romance, which promised women so much – and still do? Not from the films; we lived too far from the cinemas. Not from girls' comics either. Anyway, I had wanted to be a boy when I was little!

None of the men I worked with on the farm or met at the local village shops – Canadian Air Force, Free French, Czechoslovak and US servicemen as well as British servicemen and men from the local farms – were any kind of poet or intellectual; they were not at all like David.

Many years later I read a theory about girls who grow up without knowing their fathers, and how they seek out male approval indiscriminately in adulthood by ready response to any sexual advances. I remember the shock of recognition as I read that passage, forced to confront the possible source of my own motivations and experiences. Only my fear of pregnancy set limits on my sexual experiences.

But in May 1945, when everyone else was dancing round the bonfires on the top of the Malvern hills to celebrate VE day, I lay in the arms of a GI ... I remember that lovely early summer dusk ... the end of the war in Europe. The shock of Hiroshima was still to come.

By now my twin sister was married. I envied her. 'I'm not ready yet!' I said when people asked me about 'settling down'. That was my public answer, but in my heart I wondered whether I would ever find anyone to love me enough to marry me – not being as pretty or as successful with boys as my twin sister. I tried to be different from her because people frequently muddled us up. I wanted my life to be different from my mother's also. She had made a disastrous marriage to escape from housekeeping for a tyrannical father. Now she worked hard as a village postmistress and she looked to my sister and me for her happiness.

When I met Harold, a British airman, it was not love at first sight, but when he said 'I want to be David to you,' my heart leapt. I should have known better. I expected impossible things of him. When I thought I was pregnant we got engaged (the pregnancy turned out to be a false alarm). The war was over. I had left the WLA and was doing a two-year course in Dairying at Aberystwyth. Dairying has always been in the women's sphere, I was surrounded by women again, and how I missed their company when I left to get married to Harold.

We moved in with Harold's Mum and Dad. I was desolate and lonely. My new husband went back to his job in the Council offices and expected to live the same life as when he was single. Table tennis was his main interest. I grew tired of watching matches so I started going to adult education classes – psychology, philosophy, politics – and there made new friends of my own.

We began to go our separate ways. I realised early on what a mistake I had made in getting married, but I found a job and we got our own flat. When I gave up work three years later in 1950, to have our first daughter, we were very hard up, with no phone, no car and no prospects of owning a home. By the time our fourth daughter was born in 1959 we were able to buy our own house, not with savings – we had none – but with a small legacy from my mother's farming side of the family.

To have *four daughters*, to keep on having daughters, seemed perfectly natural to me. Other people felt sorry for Harold; surely he wanted a son? As the girls grew up he began to withdraw from being part of the family. He stayed in bed at weekends and needed more and more looking after because of his asthma. He became like a fifth child. Perhaps because my own father had been absent I made it work out the same way in my own family. I am sure I *did* nag! He was not David to me, nor ever could have been. Nor was I the wife he wanted – a younger version of his mother plus sex. It took me many unhappy years to realise that each of us was expecting the other to fulfil all needs! I was angry. I could not forgive him and I had to punish him; and I could not forgive myself for marrying him. Poor Harold! He withdrew further into illness and away from the family. He gave up the idea of studying for professional qualifications which I had nagged him about. And I? I needed the attention, if not the approval, of other men and I found consolation in a series of short and shameful affairs which I would prefer to forget.

I moved into a separate room. Gradually 'we' – my daughters and I – found it easier and easier to exclude Dad from our lives. He did not seem to notice, as long as one of us was there to serve his meals or to wait on him when he stayed in bed.

To some people the 1960s was the decade of permissiveness – long hair for men, the pill for women, the Beatles and moral decline. But I remember the 1960s as a New Age! At 38, with my daughters aged between four and 14 years old, I started on a degree course in Social Sciences at the new University of York. I got a grant and a cheque book of my own, enough to pay for some help with the family and housework. I found the course difficult – but so exciting! I struggled with essays late at night when the girls were in bed and whenever exams came I was desperate for more free time. By 1966 I had an Upper Second in Economics and Politics, then a Research Fellowship for three years.

The girls left home one by one to go on to university. The early 1970s was a good time for me to be looking for a job in adult education as it was before the days of cuts and when adult education was still expanding. There was little competition when I was interviewed for my last job, in 1971, as Lecturer in the Adult Education Department of Durham University. Now, in the 1990s, there would be hundreds of applicants.

Working with women on courses like New Opportunities for Women, Women Writing, Assertiveness, and so on, was the most satisfying and fulfilling work I have ever done. It would not have been possible without the Women's Movement and the experience of women talking together about their own lives and learning from each other that 'the personal is political'.

I left my husband in 1980, after 33 years of marriage, and we divorced by mutual consent two years later. We made the necessary arrangements amicably enough in the end. I got a mortgage on a little house of my own and he stayed on in the family home. For the first time in my life I was *free*. I had my own home, near my work at last. I invited friends in or stayed out late, putting the world to rights.

Harold died in 1984. The girls had established new and separate relationships with him and had taken it in turns to visit him at weekends. Perhaps they were only just getting to know him when he died.

I didn't go to the funeral. I was sad that his life had ended so but I felt that I had done all the grieving, shed all my tears for his loss, years before. I had found it hard to be the devoted wife in the circumstances that marriage imposes on women. My life would have been unbearable, however, without my four daughters, and now I find it hard to answer their questions: 'Why did you marry him?' 'You must have loved him once, didn't you?' I believe they understand at least some of the reasons for our divorce. I think they will cherish some happier memories of their father than I have of mine.

When I was young I was told that women are petty, spiteful, and jealous, make bad bosses and betray their women friends for men. I learned that nothing important or enjoyable happens without men. What nonsense! Isn't it other women to whom we turn for our closest friendships, and who help when we most need it?

The older I get the more I value womens company. This is what brought me to the Hen House. As for 'Growing Old Disgracefully' – I've been saving it up. It has taken a lifetime's learning to get here!

Mary

NAME: **Maxine Myers**
BORN: Maxine Adele Rachofsky
TO: Noah Rachofsky and
        Beatrice Myers Rachofsky
        of Dallas, Texas, USA

Once upon a time in a faraway land noted for its oil wells and cowboys, a woman-child emerged from a warm protective womb into an unfamiliar world not of her own making. She spent the next 60 years trying to adjust herself to this alien milieu, or it to her, she was never quite sure which. And that, gentle people, is the story of my life.

Here are a few memories and impressions from that first 60 years. I leave it to you to make sense of it all because I find it hard to see how that babe who was born into an urban working-class family of Jewish Texans could have turned out to be a Californian, an academic, a strong feminist activist and a grandmother of six.

My earliest memory seems to have two events jumbled up together: my baby sister arrived and I was given a pet baby goat. Of the two I remember more about the goat. He was my favourite playmate until he grew so big that he would accidentally hurt me when we romped together. One day my father took him away and I never saw him again (the goat, not my father). At the time I probably wished he would have taken away the new baby instead. I can say that now because even though I thought my sister Rosalee was a nuisance when we were little, we became very close in adulthood and developed a deep love for each other. Her death a few years ago was a great loss to me.

Although my father appeared to be very non-demanding, he controlled our household with a passive-aggressiveness that kept us all walking on eggs. My mother catered to him and protected him and loved him dearly. I have no doubt he loved us although like most men of his era there was little display of affection. The only recollection I have of spending time with him was when he would drive Rosalee and me to Sunday School while my mother and grandmother stayed home to prepare the big Sunday meal. On the way back we would stop at the Jewish bakery and delicatessen and the car would fill with the smells of fresh breads, dill pickles and salami. We would arrive home with our goodies and start 'noshing' while Mama fussed that we would spoil our appetites. By the time we had finished the luscious pies that Grandma had baked we were well-sated. It was my favourite day of the week.

My mother, known to everyone as Bede, was brought up in a small West Texas ranching town where she learned to drive a car before most girls had their first bicycles. Her smile was infectious and she had a sort of childlike naïvety that was endearing. To Bede, a stranger was merely someone she had known less than two minutes.

Like many women who must care for a family during desperate economic times, she was an excellent manager. For example, she would ask the butcher for leftover scraps which she would make into a tasty meal for us to eat before my father came home. She would serve him a proper piece of meat and when he asked 'what did you and the children eat?' she would assure him that we had meat also. She never lied but shielded him from pain and guilt and kept him from getting angry. From her I learned exceptional skills in resource management; I also learned that women protect men's feelings and avoid conflict at any cost.

The neighbourhood we lived in was a model of co-operation and mutual support. Children were sent out of all the houses to play with each other, to use our imaginations, to create our own games and activities. Older children looked after younger ones, and there was always somebody's mother or grandmother to call on if we needed help.

Our street was in the shadow of a vile-smelling soap plant and there were days in the scorching Texas summers when the stench was awful. I can still picture us, a pack of hot, dusty kids running after the ice-wagon to snitch slivers of ice that fell off the blocks being delivered to our refrigerator-less houses. There was something special about the smell and taste of that ice. Funny how tastes and smells evoke such strong memories.

Often pedlars came through the streets hawking fruits and vegetables and the women would run out of their houses when they heard the bell. The ragman made regular rounds looking for discards. Just around the corner was the dairy where we went to fill our metal milk-cans, and next to that was the Holy Rollers storefront church where the segregated Negroes, as they were called then, came to pray, sing and shout. Our parents forbade us to go there, so of course we went as often as we could.

School presented no challenge for me academically. I got my share of attention by making good grades while my sister was charming everyone with her sweet dimpled smile and Shirley Temple curls. She grew up thinking she was not smart and I grew up thinking I was ugly, both erroneous assumptions that plagued us into adulthood.

As leisure time activities shifted from neighbourhood free play to school dances and parties, I was the proverbial wallflower. I hated being unpopular but I pretended I was above it all. In fact, pretence became my form of resistance. I developed strategies for showing people what they wanted to see while nurturing my real thoughts and feelings inside myself. I was a Jew in the Bible-belt Texas schools so I denied my heritage and 'assimilated.' I was a bright girl who learned to hide her intelligence when she found out that boys wanted girls to be less smart than themselves; I wore glasses from the age of 18 months and never developed good hand-eye co-ordination, so I learned to hide behind the equipment shed during PE classes to avoid the humiliation of never being chosen for a team. Because I could see that women who broke the rules of conformity and passivity risked consequences ranging from rejection to violence, I knew that I must learn to play my roles well in order to survive.

In my late teens I joined a budding theatrical troupe and for the next few years my life consisted of working at a bank all day, rehearsing or performing half the night, and then going to the local popular drive-ins for hamburgers, greasy chips and drinks. I suppose it was youth that saved me, because after an hour or two of sleep I would catch the trolley and be back at work to start the pattern again.

Some of our actors went on to fame and fortune in the entertainment industry. I was not among their number. At the worldly-wise age of 21 years, I left my parents' home and moved to Los Angeles, California. For a while I worked at a bank near the famous corner of Hollywood and Vine, but that is as close as I ever came to stardom.

When I met the man who later became my husband, I was sure he was Prince Charming come to take me away from the life of a poor working girl. My parents breathed a sigh of relief, too. Beyond their wildest expectations, I was marrying a Jewish medical student. I was set for life, finally on a path they could recognise.

Ten months after the wedding I gave birth to our first son, Matthew; 17 months after that, our daughter Margo arrived; and before she turned two, Joel was born. I was caring for three children in nappies while my husband struggled to finish all his medical training.

As I start to write about this part of my life, I find myself losing the warm feelings of nostalgia I felt while writing about my childhood. It's not that everything about married life was bad, and I do believe that the first years we spent in getting established and watching our children thrive were challenging but rewarding. And I guess we didn't do too badly as parents because all three grew up to be wonderful, kind, competent, caring adults and good parents to their own children.

I think we had problems but the demands of everyday life kept us from ever looking at our own relationship. We played our roles well: I as wife and mother, he as provider. We moved to a beautiful small town, borrowed money for a down payment on a modest house which we added to and remodelled ourselves. Our lives became enmeshed with the community as we worked in local politics, schools and civic groups. I like to think that we provided our children a healthy physical and social environment, a strong base from which to launch their own lives.

As my husband became more and more successful in his profession and his many other endeavours, I expected to find his successes validating for myself, and in some ways I did. It was fun to be the mayor's wife, the behind-the-scenes helpmate, the person who made it all possible for him to carry on. But as I think back on my small acts of subversion I know that I was longing to grow as a person in my own right.

Who can tell at what exact moment a marriage begins to deteriorate beyond repair? I only know that for years we used alcohol as a way to numb the feelings and preclude honest communication. I knew I was not getting what I needed but I had no skills or practice in asking. For a while we kept up a pretence for appearances' sake, but after a night of violence when he battered and terrorised me, I knew it was time to call an end to our 15 years together.

After the divorce and a few painful years of fighting over money and custody, I started working part-time and taking some courses at the local community college. I decided to leave behind my hippy flower-child rock-concert phase into which I had escaped. I needed to build a life for myself as a single mother, and prepare myself for the day when the children would be gone. I moved back to Los Angeles for a few years to take a University degree, then came to my present home, Santa Cruz, to do graduate studies. Twelve years after my very first college class I became Dr Maxine White.

I have stayed in Santa Cruz for 13 years. I am the Director of a college Women's Centre and I teach Women's Studies, a job which provides me with much satisfaction as I watch students carving a path for themselves. I am pleased that I can contribute to their process. I have developed an identity and a reputation quite separate from anyone else's and I feel good about that.

Even though I like the life I lead, I still try to find ways to keep from becoming too set in my ways. That is why in 1989 I was looking to put a bit of what my friend Virginia and I used to call 'madness' back into my life. I was in the process of ending a ten-year relationship and had made plans to go on a women's study tour of Scandinavia when I happened to see a brochure from the Hen House. I made a spur-of-the-moment decision to sign up for the 'Growing Old Disgracefully' course and so began a new chapter in my move towards authenticity.

SHIRLEY

Looking back from the vantage point of where I am now, I can see my life as part of a continuum of escaping steps, away from the narrowness of my parents and their history. Each step has taken me further from their life-style to a synthesis of values which is my own and which avoids their inflexibility within a time warp of rigid expectations of 'proper' behaviour.

At 24, three years into a marriage which was both romantic and traditional, my husband and I took a deliberate step to reject a close-knit Jewish family life to try to determine our own path. It felt like an escape when we left London for the cold, steel-furnace fumed air of north Lincolnshire – heathen lands in our parents' eyes whose main worries for us were that we would be able to buy neither kosher meat nor cornflakes. We were excited to be exchanging the possessive intimacy of the family community for the opportunity of living among young couples at the outset of their careers, like us, and who came from all walks of life, countries and religions, and who had enthusiasms and energies quite unfamiliar from those we had so far experienced.

My husband escaped from a low-level, secure Civil Service job to which he had been directed by family with penurious experiences of unemployment in the 1930s. With my support and encouragement he had just graduated from the London School of Economics and was now part of the steel industry. I used my work as a journalist to nose around, finding those with common interests. The local careers officer and the museum curator provided both good news stories and life-time friendships. We were unfettering ourselves from parental pressures, and beginning to break new ground.

But my parents too had tried to break free from some of the limitations of their own conditioning. They had been born in the East End, that haven for immigrants from the pogroms of East Europe, from which their own parents came. My grandparents, only one of whom I knew, were illiterate in the English language and uneducated, and both my parents had to leave school at age 12 to support their widowed mothers. My maternal grandmother's only other support was the synagogue of which my grandfather had been Rabbi in the few years between arrival in Britain and death at age 40. My paternal grandmother, widowed from her pedlar husband when my dad was born, took in washing to survive.

Instead of following a common route of poor Jews into tailoring or small business, my dad escaped to London Transport as a menial white-collar office boy. He advanced, via evening classes, from draughtsman to chief cartographer, and his maps and posters adorned

London's Underground for many years. He earned very little, but somehow the self esteem he acquired from being 'professional' partially compensated. And he was proud to do air warden duty on the roof of their head offices throughout the Blitz and to sing in the chorus of all the Gilbert and Sullivan operas put on by their dramatic society. My hard-working mother, however, while basking in the glory of his autographed maps, continued to long for riches. He remained a very modest man to the end and his attitude helped me later to forego the flimsy glamour and high potential income of my career in journalism for something more intrinsically satisfying.

My parents' marriage was a bitter one, a model I rejected when my own went sour after 25 years. That earlier decision to flee the enclosed family had created an alternative concentration on our marriage that required each of us to be all things to each other. Frequent career hopping meant moves from Lincolnshire to Wales and to two different homes in Essex and this prevented the establishment of other reliable support networks. We failed to satisfy each others' needs and gradually our values and ambitions diverged. With the negative example of our parents' unhappy marriages, we decided that life was too short to repeat this pattern. So at 45, some happy years and increasingly unhappy ones of marriage behind me, he left and I escaped into the world of the single woman, though at first it felt like a retreat, fearful as I was of survival in every sense. Having anticipated the break-up I was already working full-time in London, while living with our adolescent sons in Essex, until each in turn left for university.

Coincidentally, my father's lingering death from cancer two years earlier had also triggered another point of change in my life. He had died frustrated with unfulfilled dreams. If only he had not put them off for the retirement he did not live to enjoy. No such regrets for me, I decided. I had long wondered at the cynical, beer-swilling, foot-in-the-door journalist I was becoming. Did I really want to continue in this way, in the one life I could inhabit? I had left school at 17 and had entered the world of work as the conventional secretary, inching my way forward to the lower rung of journalism by ingenuity and opportunism.

Having supported my husband through two degrees and with both sons heading towards theirs, I decided that my time too had arrived. I needed to underpin some of my intuitive skills with a more secure base if I was to feel good about myself. So, with the launch in 1971 of the Open University, I embarked on a six-year degree course, simultaneously enduring the penultimate years of a failed marriage, an acrimonious separation and divorce, and a new job as Accommodation Officer at the then North London Polytechnic. There I was responsible for housing 3,000 students annually, running the whole service of acquiring and managing hostels, private digs, council accommodation, dealing with grasping landlords, over-protective parents, overbearing bureaucracy and sometimes irresponsible student tenants.

The daily commuting distance between home and work was 30 miles and I either drove or went by train. Either way, the journey took more than one and a half hours each way. In the lunch hour I would shop for food which would weigh on my knees on the crowded train going home − if I was lucky enough to get a seat. On top of the shopping I would balance my latest OU unit in the hope that something would sink in. Not surprisingly, I lasted only six months of the fourth year before withdrawing from the course. I tried to continue the next year but failed again. As I had three credits under my belt I decided to give myself a break from failing which only reinforced my sadness. I hoped to resume it again when my life was less frantic and disturbed some time in the future. I was exhausted from a 12-hour day of work and travel and my time with my adolescent sons was limited and precious. I look back with bewilderment at how I coped and how they held on despite such adverse circumstances. Yet they did and succeeded in becoming well-balanced individuals – obtaining good degrees while entering into a full social life which included music-making, politics and friend-ships.

By 1978, with both sons at university, I had moved into London and into another job in a multi-cultural further-education college with students of all ages. Here I was working within a counselling and advice team, dealing with the wider aspects of student difficulties, family breakdown, sexuality, poverty, intercultural and race conflicts. What a lot I learned. All my remaining stereotypical images exploded.

I was escaping still further from being the conventional wife and from the standards and expectations of my upbringing. I had even dared – to the distaste of my mother – to move back into the inner city from which my parents had worked hard to escape as part of the upwardly mobile process.

By 1980 I felt positive enough to attempt to complete my degree. By 1984 – 13 years after I had started it – I had succeeded not only in obtaining it but also in completing a three-year counselling qualification. My already qualified sons shared my fully-gowned graduation ceremony with glee. My work and studies had brought me into contact with minds that stretched mine wide open and into a world with a wide range of women who were successful in going it alone without men as props, and who were constantly challenging society's norms. If I'd wanted to become complacent, their example and challenge helped me to continue growing, to gain self-confidence.

As a single traveller I had now crossed the USA coast-to-coast by Greyhound bus to celebrate my half-century and had visited China and Russia at their times of political awakening. I was swept along with enthusiasm for life. I retained friends from a wide variety of relationships, work, study and play. I was content living alone, mending my own fuses, managing my own finances, remaining available to my sons on a now more evenly balanced friendship basis. I was enjoying my freedom. What had seemed at first like a retreat, had become an escape into a life that was both happy in the present and in looking forward. By the age of 59 I had acquired some skills for the freelance work I needed to do in retirement; both my sons were happily partnered and I had acquired two impressive and caring daughters (followed since by delicious grandtwins!). Even my relationship with my ex-husband was more tolerable.

The quality of my life had been transformed by a series of escapes: from family and marriage into education, the sisterhood of women and the wider, fascinating world; from my parents' backward-looking 'if-only' life of regrets into one of non-blameful but increased self-awareness and continual development. My life was no longer contained within a closed world of old values, stale marriage and ignorance. Life ahead was full of excitement not foreboding, full of so many opportunities for stimulation and, most important, new friendships. It was in this mood, one year before retirement at 60, that I was attracted to the idea of 'Growing Old Disgracefully'.

Shirley

CHAPTER TWO

From the Dolls' House

The woman said with pride, conferring on my grand-mother the highest honour, 'Kept the house spotless, she did.' I can't bear to think of that as her epitaph.

Eryl Smith Maudsley,
Hen House participant

By and large, we women who are 'getting on a bit' as one friend euphemistically puts it, grew up in a time when keeping a spotless house with a spotless husband and spotless children was supposed to represent our highest achievement, an ideal against which we measured ourselves. As little girls we were given toys that would help us to practise the art of proper housekeeping and mothering. The dolls' house was our symbol for women's ideal existence, and we looked forward to having our own real house when we were old enough to marry Prince Charming.

Prescriptions for our proper behaviour as females came from many sources, including teachers, religious leaders, our peers and the media. Our primary socialisation, however, came from our families. It was from people associated with 'home' that we learned most of the rules. And we learned them well. We knew that women who did not fit an acceptable mould would suffer the consequences. They were socially ostracised objects of pity and scorn. You probably remember some of the epithets: fallen woman, old maid, kept woman, spinster, 'manly' woman. We knew that in the eyes of our families and of society, any marriage was better than no marriage, any man better than none.

Of course there were always exceptions, independent women who chose their own paths and set their own agendas. But most of us tried to follow the rules (or pretended to) even when they contradicted our own intuition. We thought we were making our own choices, when in reality we did not even know we had options, and once committed to a marriage we thought it would be for ever.

But then, to quote Eryl Smith Maudsley again, '. . . there is often a sudden moment of recognition when we begin to feel that, while home may be the centre of our lives, it should not be the boundary.' For some of us that recognition came early, for others it is just beginning. We are still trying to discover just how far we can expand the boundaries – which is what led us to the Hen House, to the Growing Old Disgracefully course, which we will describe in Chapter 3.

Clear Out Old Messages

One of the things we are learning is that, in order to grow old disgracefully, you must first exorcise your demons and discard old patterns that are getting in the way. They only take your precious time and energy away from creative, joyful experiences. Hanging on to old identities that are no longer valid can cause you to become terribly disappointed and frustrated. It can turn you into an old bore. That is why, in this chapter, we take you 'backstage' of our auto-biographies to identify some of the old messages we have carried around with us. Once they are identified we can get on with clearing them out. We have included descriptions of some of our early role models, our socialisers, and characteristics we developed as a result of the time and age to which we belonged. We also look at people and experiences that influenced us in ways which made it possible for us to reach old age with a positive attitude. We hope that looking back critically at these models and making choices about accepting or rejecting them will allow us to live as we want in the present, making our decisions based on what is appropriate for us now. Since none of this would have been possible without women's political struggles, we have included some writings about lessons we have learned from the contemporary Women's Movement and from women of younger generations.

We have used the theme of the dolls' house, with its different meanings for each of us, because it so powerfully represents what we have left behind. When we first sat down to discuss this concept we found that each of us had an immediate strong reaction, but for different reasons. For some of us a dolls' house evokes lovely memories of childhood; others remember our early dreams of an ideal marriage in our own ideal house; for others it feels restrictive and we picture ourselves locked in our dolls' house, yearning for something more (the Nora of Ibsen's drama). These are our impressions, yours might be different. Before you go on to read our versions, we encourage you to take a minute to think about the symbolic meaning the image has for you, and what feelings are present when you visualise a dolls' house.

Moving On

For those of you who feel stuck in old patterns of behaviour that are no longer appropriate, here is a list of suggested questions you might begin to ask yourself. They are sure to trigger more of your own. If possible, discuss your thoughts about them in a group. The goal is not to dwell on the past but to use the insights to see how you might want to adjust your attitudes and your activities to be more in line with your situation now. Ask yourself whether it is time to set new agendas while you still have the choice. As you read our writings think about:

● How and from whom did you learn what it means to be a woman? A woman over 60?

● What stereotypes of old women did you see reflected in the media when you were growing up?

● What stereotypes do you see now?

● Who were the people and what were the events that most influenced the paths you have taken?

● What was your mother like when she was the age you are now? In what ways are you like her? What do you do differently? What circumstances are similar? What has changed? Think of the same questions in relation to your grandmother or an aunt.

● Have you known someone in your life who has encouraged you to take risks, break moulds, expand your horizons?

● Who are your role models now?

● What sort of role model are you?

● Finally, how would you like to be remembered in your epitaph? If you were to write your life story, what would you want to be able to say about next week, next year, ten years from now?

As we have suggested, your autobiography can help you to see where you have been, and who and what you consider the major influences on your life, the specific circumstances that helped shape your character. It can also reveal gaps, help you to identify what is missing that could be added before the final paragraph is written. Learning from the past is one way to understand the present, but it is never an excuse for limiting your future.

MY DOLLS' HOUSE *Barbara*

My dolls' house existed only in my dreams. In my dream dolls' house there would be a mother doll, in her apron, in the kitchen, always available for the baby doll's needs; there would be a father doll, who went off to work each morning and came home to play with his children in the evenings; and there would be at least two children. I could never decide whether there would be two girl children (I longed for a sister) or a girl and a boy – the boy, of course, being the elder and always there to protect his little sister. I had learned all the lessons well and was quite clear about the rightness and desirability of this image. It could not have been more different from the reality of my life as a child. I had no father, no siblings. My mother went out to work and we lived in two furnished rooms. It is easy to see why the dolls' house held such magic for me.

When I was about 12 a local store held a raffle and the first prize was a truly wonderful dolls' house. It may be that memory has enhanced its glories but I remember it as having electric lights, and even running water which was fed from a small tank in the roof. The cost

of a raffle ticket was more than my week's pocket money but I saved every penny until I could buy a ticket. I *knew* that I was going to win that dolls' house because my longing for it was so desperate. I was a solitary child and I could visualise the hours I would spend reorganising the furniture and planning the lives of my family. But, needless to say, I did not win the raffle and I never owned a dolls' house.

Although I went straight from school to university the image of the dolls' house must have stayed locked in my heart. I could not wait to marry and to establish a family within its own four walls. By the time our third child was born we were living in a little square detached house just like a dolls' house. I had two little boys and the third was a girl – my dreams had come true! And little mummy-doll bustled around, cleaning and cooking, washing and ironing, looking after the doll-children, while daddy-doll went off to work with his brief-case and came home to play with the doll-children.

I have moved a long way since then, but the emergence from my dolls' house was a hard, painful experience. Those four walls comforted me and made me feel safe. I knew who I was within them because I was defined by my roles of wife and mother. Maybe if I had not been forcibly evicted, I would be inside the walls still. But then I would have missed some wonderfully rich friendships and unexpected adventures.

A HUFF AND A PUFF AND I'LL BLOW YOUR HOUSE DOWN *Shirley*

My son gave me a birthday present of a smoke alarm and a beautiful Matisse print, the latter only 'on condition I inherit it when you die'. The dual message of those gifts and the teasing humour that accompanied them is typical of our relationship. That he could say such a thing to me is something I would never have dared say to my mother, for fear of being 'disrespectful'. All was deadly serious all the time, missing out on the fun we could have had together, even during the hard times of the 1930s, and the Second World War in which I grew up. I know what sort of mother-child relationship I prefer – and which is healthier.

My mother and I were never friends, as I am with my children. She brought me up to remind me constantly to respect her, which created distance, and to observe two standards of behaviour: the one which faced the world and was for show, and the other within the family which, however miserable, should never be disclosed outside the walls of home. A bit like the dresses she made – which were beautiful on the outside but badly finished on the inside. We had to show calm and beauty to others whatever the emotional turmoil within the family.

So, when I think of a dolls' house it has a handsome exterior but inside there is disarray and it clearly represents the hypocrisy and the clash of my parents' standards with often vicious quarrelling at home but the representation of a contented married pair for the world to see. It was a fragile dolls' house which could be blown down by a puff of wind. My home would need stronger foundations than that.

That was the model of married life I inherited – together with that of my father as gentle, loving and artistic but a doormat to my bossy mother who was strong, energetic, loyal and ambitious, but without softness or humour.

Where I found my own sense of humour and daring is a mystery. It must have come from my peers and my school-teachers. The latter were divided between the prim spinsters and the daring ones who drove to school on motorbikes and whom I might bump into out of school in clothes quite different from the dull uniformity within school. Those few teachers who had to be addressed as 'Mrs' were the exception and thus I learned that teaching as a career must contain some sort of contagion to keep far from if I was to marry and have children, which was the conventional aspiration of my parents. The teachers were either skinny or with ample bosoms and nearly all had their hair drawn tightly back into buns. Clearly that was not for me, a choice of career that I ticked off early from my list. My teachers got my respect but in no way did I want to resemble them and condemn myself to singledom.

What other choices were there for me? There seemed no point in wasting long years studying, even if my parents could or would have wanted to support me, if my chief expectation was to marry, have kids and live happily ever after in domesticity.

Yet I was a teenager in the 1940s, whose missed adolescence had largely been spent, it seemed, in one type of air raid shelter or another at school or at home, and there was no other life between. This was another sort of unhappy dolls' house where all the games were deadly serious. While others huddled in the Underground for protection and sometimes enjoyed the camaraderie of fellow sufferers, my family isolated itself under metal-caged tables or brick-built sheds where we had survival needs from chamber pots to iron rations and where our only light relief was competition between the drips of condensation that raced down the streaming walls. Ironically, one of the rare moments that made me laugh at the time was the sight of the gingerbread impression I had made in the snow when I threw myself down to avoid a falling doodlebug on the way home from school. I was shaped by the war which denied me my adolescence just as my parents' attitude to money and security was shaped by living through the 1930s, wondering who next would be 'laid off'.

My daring deeds were limp attempts to break out of the stiff attitude of my parents – cycling downhill with no hands, telling fibs to explain late arrival home from school (quite a worry to my parents when air raids were always imminent) and other 'tomboyish activities'. My contemporary idols were all such 'nice girls' doing their bit to mend other people's unhappy lives. Shirley Temple and the young Judy Garland were coupled with literary heroines who had a touch of impetuosity about them but they always got their man in the end.

It was an all-white dolls' house world of escapism. Apart from the horror of war and the Holocaust there was no political debate at home. My parents' attitude was to avoid rocking the boat, to be thankful that there was work, enough food. I was living through the period of real emancipation for women without realising the truly historic period it was. Everything was going to be better after the war, that was the popular feeling. But the significance of full enfranchisement for women, equal pay, easy access to contraception just passed me by. I just enjoyed the benefits, and it is only now, when free health care and education are at risk, that I know how much I appreciated these things for myself and my children.

The younger generation has taught me more about the facts of life, of sexism, racism, the need to be vigilant to protect hard-won political victories than I ever learnt from my formal education. My sons and their partners, my younger women friends, the students with whom I worked over many years, have taught me to loosen my sexual inhibitions, to have greater tolerance to those I do not understand. I was a late starter in the women's liberation stakes and what I now believe comes largely from these young people. I guess I am inevitably some sort of role model for them – be it good or bad – but those whom I admire most today do not just include the Indira Ghandis and Golda Meirs but my own children and their friends, the women who bring up children singlehandedly while striving simultaneously for education and career. This generation has not lived through war with a capital W, but the wars they fight are more subversive, and they need courage. I have no doubt that they possess it. And I hope that their dolls' house memories are happier ones than mine.

IN AND OUT OF THE DOLLS' HOUSE
Edith

Most people at some time in their lives have the opportunity to look back to their origins, to what was, and assess where they are at present. In attempting to see how far I have come out of the 'dolls' house', I am doing just that. I cannot see around the corner into the future but I can try to evaluate the influence of the younger generation on the behaviour patterns and attitudes that I carried over from my parents' generation. I find myself with a foot in each camp, changing but not completely discarding all I learnt at my 'mother's knee'. So that some years ago when our son who had been attending a university in the United States brought a pretty young American girl back with him one summer, I insisted they must have separate bedrooms. He could occupy his old room on the first floor and I would clear out another bedroom for her on the second floor. I suspected that their relationship had reached the intimate stage, but as far as I was concerned the proprieties must be observed and a good example set for our younger daughter. I remember this was my thinking at the time because my husband and I discussed it at length. I felt the rules had been observed; whatever occurred after we had closed our bedroom door was no longer our responsibility. Despite these strictures our son married this pretty American the following year.

It was several years later that a young man with whom our daughter had formed a relationship came to us one evening to ask our permission to set up housekeeping together. 'Is this marriage you are proposing?' asked my husband. 'Oh no', replied the young man, 'we just want to live together in one place rather than separate establishments.' We were not completely caught off guard by the old world approach to this up-to-date lifestyle. We raised all sorts of objections, were vigorous in our disapproval, but there was nothing we could actually do to restrain them. So off they went to Wales and rented an old farm cottage with an outside toilet and not a modern piece of equipment in sight. When some time later our daughter informed us she was pregnant, we naturally assumed she would now be ready to discuss plans for an early wedding. But this was not on their agenda and nothing I said was about to change their decision. I was completely shattered. My expectation for her had been so different. I had wanted for her what I couldn't have when I was growing up, but our views of life and our values didn't coincide at that point in time. However much I disapproved of this arrangement there was nothing I could do. After my Welsh granddaughter was born we visited them from time to time and had to admit that despite the absence of modern conveniences she was a beautiful, healthy baby. We also agreed that the view in the early morning, from the outside toilet, of the Brecon Hills, sometimes snowcapped, was truly magnificent.

In the intervening years I have been gradually emerging from the dolls' house, never quite abandoning all I had learned at my mother's knee, but certain that, were I confrontd with the same situations today, my responses would surely be otherwise. In part this can be attributed to the radical changes in social patterns that have taken place, but the major responsibility for my enlightenment comes from another source – my children and grandchildren. Through them I have become aware of the great variety of lifestyles in today's world and learned to be more tolerant of them, accepting my daughter's (now that of a single parent) and admiring her ability to so successfully raise her two daughters on her own. However, there is still a part of me that would like to see young people prepared to

make a long-term commitment to intimate relationships and work hard at sustaining them. It's that part of
me that keeps one foot in the dolls' house. The part
outside has found support and nourishment in women's
groups, has discovered the confidence to voice my
objections to sexist and ageist remarks, is constantly
reminding my husband that we are no longer 'girls' but
are women, and is coming to understand and provide
for her own needs. I'll probably never make it
completely outside the dolls' house but it won't be for
lack of trying.

COMING OUT OF THE AGE CLOSET
Maxine

I am 63 years old and for the first time in my life, I feel
that my age fits me. Or I fit my age. It hasn't always
been so.

All during my childhood, I looked several years older
than my actual age, and I was expected to act that way.
I was given the responsibilities and freedoms of a much
older child. Early on, I developed a fierce independence
that belied my years.

My parents, upon advice from my schoolteachers,
agreed to have me moved ahead two grades with the

consequence that throughout my academic years my classmates were always older than I. I usually lied to strangers about my age by adding on a few years to achieve congruence with my physical appearance, grade level and friends.

Having lied, or at least having omitted the truth about my age, I would then have a devilish time explaining to ticket sellers and tram conductors why I was still asking for youth fares when my friends weren't. I took to carrying my birth certificate to use on such occasions as it was to my advantage to prove that I was young, and conveniently misplacing it when I wanted the status of my peers.

My body began to mature very early. I started menstruating at the age of nine, and by the time I was 12, I was tall and full-breasted. I seemed to leap from childhood to adulthood with little or no transition. I finished school at 14, but since I was a girl, higher education wasn't considered necessary (my parents couldn't have afforded it anyway). I was too young to marry, so three months before my fifteenth birthday, I entered the job market.

I had to lie again about my age when I filled out job applications. It was wartime when any civilian who could spell her name and count to ten got hired. Since I had finished all my compulsory schooling, it was easy to convince the interviewer that I was 16 years old (the legal working age). So just before my fifteenth birthday, I began as a mail clerk at a bank, earning the grand sum of 80 dollars per month.

Given my newly-found 'wealth' I began to acquire stylish clothing, wear make-up, and adopt other fashionable trappings of the sophisticated working woman, all of which added to the illusion of maturity. I had my own charge accounts, none of which would have been approved had they thought I was under 18 and still living with my parents.

I was never popular with schoolboys, but now men were beginning to notice me. I took weekend trips with girlfriends, and flirted shamelessly with uniformed servicemen. My suitors all thought I was much older, and I did nothing to disabuse them of the notion.

Later, during the 1950s, my age seemed fairly appropriate to my activities as wife and mother, but when I divorced in 1969, just before my fortieth birthday, age suddenly seemed salient again. Because I didn't become aware of alternatives until much later, I assumed that the only way to restart my life would be to find a new husband; however, a 40-year-old woman with three children does not have great marketability in the romance department.

It was about that time that the student movements were proclaiming anyone over 30 as the enemy, and all public attention was being directed toward youth. At 42, I was in the process of taking some college courses for the first time, and I was thrown into a system designed for and populated by 18 – 21 year olds. Now, rather than being older than me, my schoolmates were half my age. Once more I was out of step.

I'd like to say that age was unimportant, and to some extent that would be true. As students we were all subjected to the same exams and assignments. I became acquainted with some wonderful young people with whom I talked, lunched, studied. Then they would go off to their parties and dates and I would go home to the responsibilities of a house, three children and two dogs. Even my teachers were younger than I.

The incongruity between my chronological age and my student status was disconcerting. To reduce the dissonance, I began to deny that I was like other women in their forties. I didn't want to be my age. I took much younger men as lovers, went to rock concerts, wore flowers in my hair, sewed long dresses from Indian bedspreads, hippie fashion, and stayed barefoot much of the year. I took great delight in hearing people say that I didn't 'look my age'.

What ageist nonsense! I was naive, unaware of the politics of age, untouched (I thought) by ageism. I was finishing my basic courses with high marks, and with a counsellor's encouragement, I had applied to and been accepted at a major university to complete a bachelor's degree. At the same time I wanted to apply for a State Scholarship to help with tuition. Stated clearly on the application form was the following: 'Available to students under 25 years of age.' CLICK!

Now, I'm hardly a person one could ordinarily call confrontational, but seeing blatant injustice makes me break through my passivity and pushes me to action. I didn't know how to use the words 'age discrimination' but I perceived the wrongness of denying aid to someone strictly on the basis of age. My first thought was to hire an attorney, but I hadn't the money, so I rang the local chapter of the American Civil Liberties Union (ACLU), an organisation that works at no charge to defend civil and constitutional rights. I left my message, explaining the problem.

Several days later I received a call from an ACLU attorney, who said that they had agreed to take on my case. In their opinion, there was not only ageism but sexism as well, since most adult returners were women who had left education to care for families. They were prepared to go to court and so was I, but the State Legislature got wind of it and quickly decided to amend the application to exclude reference to age. And yes, I received my scholarship, as well as later fellowships for graduate work.

By the time I had earned my doctorate, I was 54 years old. I found a great job, my sons and daughter were grown, and I was in a long-term relationship. I had learned much from the Women's Movement about sexism, racism, ageism, anti-Semitism and other forms of oppression. I had also begun to examine and work on my own internalised oppression, which had kept me feeling that being old was not OK. I began to reject the Jewish Mother stereotype as being sexist and anti-Semitic, and started to celebrate the strengths and courageousness of my traditions. I challenged the negative labels put on mothers-in-law, stepmothers and old women in general.

I no longer lie about my age. I have come out of the age closet. I say how old I am and it feels just right. I like calling myself an old woman – it makes me feel strong and wise and important.

Other people sometimes seem embarrassed when I say I'm old. They're quick to reassure me that I'm not *really* old, as if it were some horrible disfigurement, or a disease they're worried about catching, like being (heaven forbid) single, which I am again by choice. My life is far from perfect and I have much to learn, but I feel more authentic than ever before. I'm growing old disgracefully and enjoying each step along the way.

I am 63 years old.

LINES MY MOTHER TAUGHT ME
Mary

Now learn to be the lady
Quite demure and dressed in blue
If you stay the tomboy playmate
No man will marry you!

Now don't try to be too clever
You're the power behind the throne,
The hand that rocks the cradle –
It's a man's world, not your own!

MY MOTHER AND AUNT FANETTE
Edith

The warm glow of memory added to my own experience of mothering has helped me to see my mother
in perspective. By any standards she had a difficult,
unfulfilled life. She arrived in New York at the age of
15 with no knowledge of English, to live with relations
she knew little about and had never seen. She had left
behind in Austria a widowed mother and two younger
brothers, who were looking to her for financial
support. Not an easy beginning, but she fulfilled their
expectations, providing them with a regular income
once she was established, learnt to read and write
English, developed an interest in music and began to
read extensively. She married my father at the age of 24,
just before the outbreak of the First World War.

It was inevitable that she would be the dominant
figure in our family. She was strongly motivated with
expectations for us all. Her domination increased after
the collapse of my father's small business when she
took on the role of family provider in addition to all
her other duties. I never appreciated her difficulties
then nor the strain she was under to keep the family
going. I was primarily concerned with my own feelings
of resentment and frustration and trying to cope with
my mother's extreme behaviour swings, none of them
attractive. We all survived and in a curious way were
strengthened by the ordeal.

It is sometimes difficult to remember that my Aunt
Fanette and my mother were of the same generation,
they were so unlike one another. Just thinking about
my aunt makes me smile. When she first married, she
was plain Fanny, but not long after we were requested
to please call her Fanette. She was the outsider in my
father's family, the second wife of his older brother. I
never knew his first wife, she died when I was very

young; she had been, I was told, the perfect wife and mother – gentle, industrious, loving, an excellent cook and a wonderful housekeeper. Aunt Fanette was just the opposite, her main occupation being herself! A home-maker she was not; housekeeping was the least likely of her attributes. It was fortunate that they lived in an apartment hotel, the American equivalent to a service flat, plus a large hotel lobby. Here all the services were available, she would not need to lift a red-enamelled finger should she not wish to. She was always impec-cably groomed, from the top of her bleached marcelled head to the toes of her patent leather shoes. I can just see her sitting in the hotel foyer, a cigarette holder in her well manicured hand, deep in animated conversation with other 'ladies or gentlemen of the lobby'. On our occasional visits with my father, we would be taken up to the apartment, provided with a cold drink, then my sister and I were permitted to try on her gold earrings, bracelets and necklaces. So adorned we would stand in front of her dressing table mirror, grimacing and ges-ticulating, pretending to be film stars. We would have loved to play with her make-up, to duplicate her rouged cheeks, pencilled eyebrows and especially the movie star lips, but that was strictly forbidden. In the later years I would overhear whispered gossip about Aunt Fanette and her lobby companions. She was considered a disgrace by the sisters-in-law as they watched her every whim catered for by their besotted brother, while secretly envying this woman who was able to live her life as she chose, while they were forced to support their families as their respective husbands couldn't or wouldn't.

We enjoyed our infrequent visits with her. She wasn't ill-natured or bad tempered, just self-centred. I never thought of her as someone I would wish to emulate in later years. She was, in that period, a temporary escape from the greyness of my life into a more colourful and cheerful world.

Unlike my Aunt Fanette, many women of my mother's generation were working wives not through choice but from necessity. They might be in occupations requiring a special skill, like dressmaking, or it could be selling either in their own small shop or behind someone else's counter, rarely in a profession except for teaching. My mother was involved in both selling and sewing made-to-measure curtains. She carried on with this speciality into her late sixties, only abandoning it when she could no longer cope with the weight of the draperies.

It was in the latter years after the death of my father, that she spent long summers with us in London, escaping the intense New York heat. With no financial concerns, she was finally able to relax and enjoy family life. It was then that our children came to know her well. She would sit in the garden, chatting with our son and daughter or whoever came to visit; her hands always busy either knitting for us or embroidering a tablecloth or napkin. She developed a close relationship with my unmarried daughter, being able to withhold judgement about her way of life as she had never been able to do with me. When my daughter's first child was born in Wales, my frustrated mother, unable to visit or speak with her, gave vent to her feelings with 'I don't mind anything – her not being married – but not to have a telephone, that I can never understand'.

A MEMORY *Barbara*

Where was it – a fête or a bazaar? I can't remember. I must have been about six years old, it was very crowded and grown-up rears pressed in on all sides. I stopped for a moment, let go of my mother's hand and I lost her. Oh horrors, where was she? I had lost my mummy!

Suddenly, through a gap in the rumps I saw a familiar well-corseted rear covered by a flowered print silk dress, and a familiar black handbag, held in the crook of a bent elbow. I squirmed through the crowd and, grasping the free hand, looked up with relief at ... a stranger's face.

It was not until years later that I realised that my mistake arose because my mother was wearing the uniform for young matrons of the day. Corsets, well-boned brassieres, slips, stockings with seams that must be straight up the centre of the calf, high-heeled shoes with handbags to match and neat, tidy, un-sexy frocks. (Frock is a word which seems to have disappeared along with this concept. My mother-in-law always wore frocks but my mother moved with the times and learned to call them dresses.) No wonder I mistook another woman for my own mother, there must have been dozens of similarly dressed women there that day.

This was the image of womanhood offered to us when we were girls, the uniform for the housewife and mother for all social occasions. We like to believe that we are free of such uniformity, that we make our own choices. I wonder if that is true, or are the tracksuits, loose pants and T-shirts, the short hair and flat shoes which we choose to wear just as much the uniform of today's women as the frocks, high-heels and matching handbags were for our mothers?

MY AGED CHILD *Barbara*
(written on the day my mother died, aged 94)

It has been too easy
This relationship of ours
Mother-daughter, daughter-mother,
Too easy because too little has been said,
Cocooned within your confidence
You neither saw nor heard
My pain, my need.

Where were you when I needed you?
Why could we never speak?
I needed you, I needed you to hear.
Years, years ago I should have cried,
Shouted, screamed 'hear me!'
Instead I wrote your shopping lists
Washed, ironed, chatted,
And the wall between us,
The invisible glass wall,
Thickened and grew higher.

And then you became my child
And I could reach out to touch you.
'Don't be afraid. I am here for you,
You who were never there for me.'
My aged child. I held your hand
And brought you sweets.
You needed me and I was there for you
And, in the end, was that enough?

For I am left with such a sadness
Such a sense of loss.
Not loss of a relationship
But of an unfilled vacuum.
I wish … I want … I need … I miss…
What? What? WHAT? WHAT?

THREE GENERATIONS   *Barbara*

Generalisations usually lead to over-simplification; life is more complex than abstract assumptions allow for. But by looking at our individual stories we can see that there are factors which are common to all of us and changes in society which have influenced all our lives and brought us into a new relationship with the world both inside and outside our homes.

My grandmother was a poor immigrant in a foreign country; her command of English was limited and over a period of 18 years she endured 13 pregnancies from which ten children survived. Her seven daughters grew up in the East End of London, each of them leaving school at the earliest possible date to find a job and bring some money into the family. My grandmother died when she was 64 after a life of stoical endurance.

My mother was the fifth child and the sixth was born 18 months later. She cannot have received much mothering. She had little education but she was a great reader, she loved Shakespeare and had a prodigious memory for poetry which lasted until the end of her life. After a tragically short marriage she had to work to support herself and me, at a time when society did nothing to help a single parent. But nevertheless, she was able to achieve a much better life than her mother had ever dreamed of. She had a tremendous zest for life, a great capacity for enjoyment and never bemoaned her fate. Just before she died, aged 94, she said 'I have had a good life. I've been so lucky.' But, to be honest, she was not a good mother because her own needs always came first, often at my expense. And modesty was not one of her qualities. She had unbounded conceit which made it hard to love her.

How different has my life been from that of my grandmother and my mother? The gulf between us is enormous; for me, as for many other women, access to higher education in the post-war years created a break with past patterns which changed my expectations in ways which previous generations of women could not have believed possible. I stayed on at school until I was 18, then went straight to university on a scholarship of £250 a year. (This may not sound much but when I married in 1951 my husband, a qualified architect, started work at £600 a year so my grant made a large contribution to our budget.) I don't think we realised what a privileged generation we were in those early post-war years. Education was no longer only for the rich or exceptionally brilliant, it was ours as a right. And with education came changing perceptions about work, equality, politics and our lives. There were many other changes which benefitted women at that time: the National Health Service gave our babies a better start in life, the Welfare State provided help for single parents, the sick and unemployed, and family allowances put some money into the pockets of women most in need. My mother's and grandmother's lives would have been very different with such help.

My grandmother can have had little time to waste on introspection and self-doubt. She must have needed all her energy to get through each day. If my mother ever had any self-doubts she kept them very securely hidden. When my children found her boasting unbearable I used to try to explain to them that she really felt insecure inside and covered this insecurity by telling us how wonderful she was. They looked at me with disbelief. Maybe it had started out like that but in the end the pretence had become the reality. She could not express emotion; she found it difficult to share feelings or to talk about fear or pain or joy with any intimacy; she never told me that she loved me.

Early on I learned that to express emotion was 'soppy', that we were not a 'kissy' family, that it was 'silly' to be moved by beauty or joy. How wonderful it was to realise that she was the one who was unnatural, that the spontaneous sharing of feelings is the best gift you can give or receive. This is something I learned when I became a mother myself, and am still learning through my women friends.

Over these three generations of women in my family, patterns changed and expectations rose and in each generation the parents felt that they should look up to their children, that they had been able to provide the base from which their children could move upwards. It was possible to be idealistic, to believe that the world would be a better place for the next generation to inherit. But what now? All the old certainties have vanished, the world is a harsher place than it was in our youth. We could feel confident that education was the key to the future but education is no longer a guarantee of employment, our children will be fortunate to maintain the standard of living we were able to provide for them. In years to come, when my grandchildren look back over the generations, I wonder what patterns they will discern and what lessons they will derive from our family history.

ROLE MODEL – MY MOTHER-IN-LAW *Shirley*

She could harbour a grudge for years and years and years like many of her sisters – but her redeeming features more than compensated. I only knew my ma-in-law as an old woman – or so it seemed, although she was in her late forties when I first met her. Her tough life of financial hardship, long working hours in the home, factory and market, her shock at seeing her home go up in flames during the war, all showed in her face. But her appearance belied her spirited personality and twinkling sense of humour which showed in her blue eyes.

She had been truly disgraceful from her earliest days, she was happy to recall. She had gone to the cinema on Saturday matinees when it was quite unacceptable for a good Jewish girl to do such a thing on the sabbath – and became an expert in false alibis in the process. She had ridden side-saddle on motorbikes in her teens, was cheeky to strangers, had sent vituperative telegrams across the Atlantic to lodgers who had misbehaved or owed her money. She enjoyed telling of her mini-adventures and created melodramas out of family life which would otherwise had been boring and banal. She could argue with the public in the best market trader style. Of course she was always in the family doghouse for her daring escapades, which were clearly an attempt to break out of externally set rules and the close-knit East-End family which also nourished her and on which she was dependent. In turn she became the pivot of the family when she became its eldest member.

She knitted her five grandsons together with close bonds that last long after her death. Her Friday night suppers, designed exclusively for them, were regular diary events that for many years became the high point of their week.

Their behaviour as adolescents sometimes bewildered her sense of propriety but she took it on the chin – for nothing was allowed to mar their interwoven relationships. She also suffered much pain and sometimes derision when her own children did not conform to family expectations. Both their divorces caused her great distress but, again, nothing was to separate her from her children, so she swallowed and carried on.

She lived on the fifteenth floor of a council tower block which sometimes swayed in the wind.

Nevertheless she concocted plastic sheeting to protect the seedlings she nurtured on her tiny balcony, much as she tended to the flocks of family, friends and their children who crowded out her tiny flat almost every day. Certain drawers had toys for the children which they could play with when there, but leave behind for the next visit. In other corners were hidden little treats they could take away. On the table would be the most marvellous meals, sweetmeats and strudel made from home-made, paper-thin pastry in a kitchen too small to swing a cat. Spare light bulbs, screwdrivers, pencil and paper, remnants and embroidery silks were each in their allotted place for their time of need and immediate discovery.

Around her walls were the embroidered pictures which were to be our inheritance 'in the fullness of time'. By her latter years, the walls were packed tightly with those scenes of Japanese gardens, flower pieces, landscapes, all of which had the name of the intended inheritor stuck tightly to the back. We all knew which was to belong to whom and she enjoyed and swelled with pride at our genuine admiration of her picture gallery, knowing that their ultimate destination would be to those she loved.

Every day to her was a bonus for she had been advised of life-threatening risks were she to have children. True to herself, she dared to have them and won through to a grand old age, despite much ill health of which she didn't complain or fuss. Life was for living and had she been born in other times, her intelligence and wit might have been put to grander, more worldly purposes. But, in her terms, the family was all. Her legacy was love and generosity – not of riches but of herself. By giving it in her lifetime, she enjoyed the richness of our love in return.

LEARNING TO BE A WOMAN *Mary*

'You look quite demure', my mother said to me approvingly, dressed up in my new young lady outfit – hyacinth blue, fitted bouclé coat and navy brimmed felt hat.

'Demure' – a word to make me laugh and cringe!

To look like a lady at 18 – tamed but serene. Was this the ideal image of a daughter my mother had of me?

Girls were expected to make a good catch – but never to be caught in the act. We had somehow to be *found*.

I didn't go to the pictures like many girls I knew, because we lived in the country, too far away from the nearest cinema. But we read old copies of *Woman's Weekly*. They were stored in the little box-stools set on either side of the hearth in my mother's friend's house. Whenever we visited we gleaned from them whatever we could about the adult women's world of sex and love and fashion. There was much more about fashion than love and more about love than sex. Fashion was something you aspired to or contrived to achieve. Love happened when you met Mr Right. You saved yourself – ie the sex – for him, but not until after the wedding bells had rung!

It was disgraceful to be unmarried.

It was also disgraceful to have a mother who was divorced way back in the 1930s. Disgraceful to have a father we knew so little about and never talked about.

The pressure from my mother was on us both – my twin sister and me – to conform, to prove from then on that we were respectable, ordinary. The message was – *never* draw attention to yourself!

During the decade of the 1950s, I married and had four children. Not much time or opportunity to be disgraceful. My mothering duties were very clearly prescribed by my mother's and mother-in-law's expectations and the opinions current at the time. I never left the children for a single night.

But by then I had a new role model – a friend of my own age who grew more disgraceful year by year. She chucked up her job as a small-town journalist, bought an old, second-hand yacht and sailed off to the South of France – picking up a crew as she went. She has never married; always had good friendships and good lovers on occasions. Now she is 70. She lives alone in a caravan – still on the French Riviera. Around the caravan she has made a garden – an arch for roses, a wooden fence and a gate, all made from odds and ends salvaged from rubbish tips. And she has three cats, well loved. She's not always happy – I know that. My friends and my daughters, who remember her may occasionally feel a pang of pity for her, but they also envy and admire her. She brought to our provincial suburban lives a wholly different world – of travel, adventure and glamour. She provided a new kind of role model for being a woman – fun to be with, well-travelled, well-read, a woman on her own. Defiant, disgraceful – a woman before her time. My generation and my daughter's generation had need of her.

In 1963 I started my life again, as a student, at 38. I was one of the older generation amongst all the 18 to 20 year olds. I learned not so much *from* them as *with* them. The 1960s were the days of student protest and power, the Days of May in Paris in 1968, of the shootings at Berkeley, of Black Power and Flower Power, of the Beatles, the Pill and the trek to Katmandu. Looking back it was a glorious time – I learned to know what I think; I learned to see the world with the eyes of the 1960s generation.

Meanwhile, back at home, my daughters were growing up. Gone were the stuffy and complacent days of the 1950s. To them the 1960s and 1970s were more about permissiveness than politics, but I still found it

difficult to discuss sex and relationships with family –
even with my own daughters. Yet I was already on their
side. So it was all right for our eldest daughter at 20 to
marry a Trinidadian, who is black; all right for our
second daughter to share a bedroom or a house with a
boyfriend, married or not. Such new freedoms for
daughters had to be negotiated not only with my
husband but also with the grandparents – though my
in-laws were never reconciled to a black husband for
their granddaughter.

I like to think of myself and of the women of my
generation as negotiators between two worlds: the old
world that our mothers grew up in, still full of
Victorian rigidities and repressions; and the new post-
war world that our daughters know, more affluent,
more liberated, more self-aware and politically
conscious than any previous generation of women. My
generation has learned from both – from the old world
and the new; to this extent we could claim to stand at
a particularly pivotal point in history.

Now that more of us than ever before survive into
old age ours is the oldest generation there has ever been
– and the greatest benefits have accrued to women like
ourselves. As late into the century as the 1920s, the
majority of women did not survive long enough after
the birth of their last child to think of growing old
disgracefully. Now that period has lengthened to 30
years and more. It is all that lies behind this one statistic
that is making the transformation of women's lives in
old age possible – the reason why we can justifiably
claim: 'We are the New Generation!'

One is not born a woman, one becomes one.
Simone de Beauvoir, *The Second Sex*

SOCIALISATION *Shirley*

I was brought up 'proper' so they say
To become a lady by night and day.
My world was full of oughts and shoulds.
What NOT to do, so that I could
Find a man to marry well
But if unhappy, not to tell.
Better any husband than none at all
Even if my back were against the wall.

I was mostly told what not to do
Not how, or what or why or who.
The messages came quite fast and plentiful
All aimed to create a wife so dutiful.

Don't hunch your neck.
Don't answer back.
Don't slurp your soup
Don't sit and mope.
Don't knife the peas
Don't cross your knees
Don't say rude things
Don't spread your wings.

Don't forget to say your prayers.
Don't tip backwards on the chairs.
Don't scuff your heels or leave hair in sinks.
And never yield to a man who winks.
Don't gulp your food and omit to say pardon
If you burp or fart. Leave bad manners in the garden.
Don't eat with your fingers nor with your knife
Remember your purpose is to become a wife.

Don't pick those horrid looking pimples
Or you'll lose your quite alluring dimples.
Don't play footsie under the table
Or you'll have a baby as soon as you're able.
Don't swear for that's not what ladies do,
They smile and answer when they're spoken to.
Speak when you're spoken to or not at all
Or you'll end a spinster in a large white shawl.

Learn to type: read shorthand with speed.
Be sweet to your boss, then marry and breed.
Have kids, a garden, make cakes, cherry pie
Then live happy ever after – and never need cry.

AND MAKE ME A GOOD GIRL *Anne*

... That was the ending of my childhood prayer to
God, formulated by my parents and said by me at
bedtime every night. No wonder I need to redress the
balance now and grow old disgracefully!

As a small child, perhaps even into my teens, I took
the phrase very seriously. All my upbringing was
focused on making me good, nice, unselfish, polite. I
successfully repressed the nastiness, rudeness and
selfishness and often hated my younger brother and
sister, elderly aunts, and all those others I was told to
be nice to. I well remember being told off by my father
for some not-very-serious misdemeanour, as I thought
very unfairly, and as he told me to go to my room I
shouted 'Go and jump in the dustbin!' I suppose I
thought he was rubbish ¿ I shocked myself by saying
anything so outspoken. I knew that children should be
seen and not heard!

Over the past ten years I have started a process of

letting go. Letting go of the ballast, of the behaviour, of the messages that are not helpful or beneficial to me. It is a hard, slow process but an exciting one and I feel that a new me, perhaps a real me, is being allowed to emerge. But the path is not without pitfalls; the past calls me back in a seductive tone from time to time.

I started by talking about prayers. In the last few months I have been on a quest to reclaim my Jewishness and my connection with the earth and all its creatures, plants and trees. I want to be versed in its magic, in the great spirit, in the wholeness and roundness of the universe. I want to know the spiritual me. I am struggling with my spirituality both as a woman and as a Jew. I can now acknowledge the shadow side of myself and, from that knowledge I can face the future with hope and anticipation. I have even started saying prayers again before I go to sleep at night, to a God who is somewhat abstract. I sometimes think that She is a special, spiritual part of myself. The content of my prayer now is very different from my prescribed childhood words, but I still have difficulty overcoming the habit of saying at the end 'And make me a good girl.'

TEACHERS ALONG THE PATH
Maxine

I was fortunate to grow up in an extended family household. My mother's parents and brother, Hymie, came to live with us while I was still very young, so while I have some memories of going to visit them out in the country, I remember a lot more about the years we shared as a family.

My Uncle Hymie loved and accepted me unconditionally, and when I reached the age of thinking that my parents were so misguided, so utterly old-fashioned, so lacking in sensitivity that they couldn't possibly understand me, it was to him that I turned for guidance. Indeed, he became like a second father to me when I left home and moved to Los Angeles to live with him and his wife Claire.

Grandpa Bill stayed on with us until his Parkinsonism got so advanced that he needed supervised care, but I think it is from him that I inherited an eagerness to go to new places and see new things. Of all the family members, however, Grandma Nellie comes to the foreground with the most clarity.

Grandma was severely diabetic and needed the care my mother was able to provide. I watched her health decline despite a strict diet and daily insulin injections. I can still see her eating a grapefruit while the rest of us had our sweets; or drinking plain soda water on our trips to the ice cream fountain. I watched her inject herself and sterilise the needles and I remember exactly what her syringe case looked like and where she kept it. What I don't remember is ever hearing her complain about her lot in life.

Grandma lost both her legs. First one was amputated, and she was fitted with an artificial leg and learned to walk again; then the other amputation left her wheelchair bound for the rest of her life. She would say

'God has been good to me. He could have taken my arms and eyes, but he left those so I can still do the things I love.' And she did – from her wheelchair she did most of our sewing, knitting, ironing, quilting and baking. We took her once a week to the neighbourhood cinema where they set aside a special spot for her chair. I would get her situated then go off to sit with my friends until the movie ended. I felt no embarrassment or resentment; I just learned to accept that being physically limited was how some people were. From Grandma I learned courage and that there was always something positive to look for in any situation. I was 14 years old when she died, still in her fifties.

There were other role models along my life's path, some positive and some negative, but there was at least one whose influence cannot be left out. My mother's cousin Eleanore probably has no idea how much her presence in my life counterbalanced my home situation. There were no books in our house and I never saw my parents go to a play or a concert or take a proper holiday. Eleanore lived close by and when I was only a tot, she began to take me with her to the Cocke School of Expression where she taught what was then called 'elocution'. It was there that I learned to read and recite poetry, using proper diction. I was taught phonetics and cleansed of my Texas drawl. I took part in the dreadful school plays that my family felt duty-bound to attend, painful as it must have been for them. I was introduced to a cultural world I never knew existed.

I have no idea who paid for my lessons, or whether Eleanore took me because she recognised my potential or just to get me out from under my mother's feet on Saturday mornings. I stayed at the school for many years, even after Eleanore left, earning my tuition by helping out with the younger students. Those years surely shaped my love of literature and theatre, although thinking back on our awful productions, it is a wonder that I was not deterred for ever.

Eleanore gave me my first real book: *The Complete Works of Robert and Elizabeth Barrett Browning*. She was my only intellectual link in a non-intellectual world. She helped me memorise poems and plays and analyse them. But there is one event I will never forget.

When I first started at the 'expression school' I was given a poem to memorise. When I was asked to get up and recite it to the others I was so terrified I was mute. Mrs Cocke – great, large, forbidding, stern Mrs Cocke – stood over my tiny self and insisted I get on with my performance; I was equally insistent that I would not. I cried. I wet my pants. She held my shoulders and would not let me leave. The others were dismissed while Eleanore waited for me. After what seemed an eternity in hell, with Mrs C. holding fast in her determination, I said my piece between racking sobs. I suppose today we would call it child abuse, but do you know what? To this day give me two or more people to listen and I will get up and perform at the drop of a hat. So who knows, do I count this as a positive or negative experience? What I do know is that Eleanore was the one who consoled me, praised me and delivered me to my parents with not a word about what happened, at least not in front of me. I think it was then that she and I really bonded and I learned what it meant to be able to trust someone.

So there you have a glimpse of some of my early role models. Perhaps I have romanticised them a bit or left out some of the negatives, but I think it is time to focus on good things I learned and to say a belated 'thank you' to all those who gave me a foundation for growing old disgracefully. Although I have lived much of my life differently from theirs and I have rejected many of their ways, I am proud of their legacies. I can only hope that my own children and grandchildren will say as much about me some day.

PRECONCEIVED SPINSTER   *Shirley*

Old spinsters are seen as figures forlorn
So lonely, pitiful, prim and careworn.
Do they sit meek and peaceful,
Remain unrevengeful
While others live fully
With broods quite unruly
Of children who play
And lighten the day?

Or maybe the spinster's got spunk, is a harridan
Who dances and flirts and enjoys quite a carry on.
Maybe she's happy, maybe she's sad,
Maybe she feels she does not need a lad.
Maybe she wants a career of her own
Maybe not wanting to speak on the phone
To a lover who grieves her
Or even deceives her.
Maybe she wants to live on her own.

Maybe she's lived disgracefully once
Is happy to dream and remember,
Maybe she has no need for a man
From January through till December.

Maybe she made a choice to forego
Married life and the pain and the show
For independence, success
Without husbands or stress.

Not every woman wants to be tied to a man
Being single may be part of her plan
To do as she wishes
To select who she kisses
Be a slob or houseproud
Keep the radio on loud
Maybe she wants to live on her own.

Why should we want her to choose otherwise?
Her life is her own, even if compromise.
Don't all women do that one way or another
With partners, employment and also our lovers?

Why should we see her as failure unwed
If she chooses to sleep alone in her bed
Or choose her own sex
However complex
If she is quite clear in her head?

MY FATHER *Anne*

My father was born in 1897, the youngest in a family of six. He was always afraid of his very authoritarian father, and he, in his turn, became an authoritarian father. He wanted my mother's sole attention, and I think he envied and resented the time and care she gave to us, her three children. He tried to impose his authority by shouting at us, and I particularly remember him at mealtimes, growling 'Take your elbows off the table', 'don't talk with your mouth full', 'eat more slowly'. If he thought we misbehaved at the table, he would throw down his napkin and storm out of the room, leaving us sitting sheepishly, not always sure what had caused the outburst.

For him, there was little spontaneity and he allowed little in us. Most important was what the neighbours, family, business friends thought. My father was a terrible prude – I remember going in to my parents' bedroom as a small child, when my father was fully dressed, and he yelled 'Don't come in while your mother is dressing!' In my teens when boy-friends saw me or came to visit, he, having gone to bed early, would yell from the top of the stairs, every five to ten minutes

'Anne, it's time you went to bed', or 'Anne, do you know how late it is?' – hardly encouraging for my startled beaux, who were trying to cuddle up or kiss me goodnight!

In later years, when I was a married woman with two children, I lent him a book which was a little risqué, but hardly pornographic. When he returned it to me, he expressed shock that I had read such 'purple' prose.

My remembered picture is of him sitting in a leather armchair in our dining-room, hidden behind a newspaper, inaccessible, unapproachable, uncommunicative.

His most lasting influence on me, apart from the need to be 'good' and 'nice', was what seemed like his terrible, overwhelming disapproval of all I did or said. I could not please him, although I tried to in many ways. This has had a profound effect on my relationships with men, because, whatever the situation, I feel disapproval. I feel put down, unworthy. My ex-husband, my son, work colleagues have all made me feel like this from time to time.

I experience a sadness and a loss. A relationship that could have been so nourishing, so sustaining, was never there. When I see young fathers now, actually enjoying their children, spending time with them, listening to them with respect, I feel unutterably sad and envious. From reading autobiographies, I sense that most women who have excelled in their professions or occupations have done so with the encouragement and belief of their fathers, or some other significant male figure, but that has changed in recent years.

My father died so many years ago, and I have grown and developed despite him, but it has been an unbalanced growth, where I don't care for or acknowledge the masculine within myself, nor do I care to spend much time in the company of men. I know of the imbalance, but it feels irreversible.

TEACHERS *Barbara*

Miss Gaunt was my Maths teacher at High School. Her name was remarkably apt, as some names are. She was tall and angular, with lank straight hair. She was an excellent teacher yet carried with her an air of failure; she was not popular, lacking the light touch to win her pupils' hearts.

She and I travelled to school by the same route, I from the terminus and she from a stop or so further on. One day the train was full by the time she got on and when I offered her my seat she insisted that I sit on her lap. Full of embarrassment I perched on her bony knee while she beamed and talked of her own childhood and how she had always loved maths – as she knew I did too.

I couldn't wait to get to school and tell my friends – 'Guess what! The Gaunt made me sit on her knee! Ugh!' But at their screams of laughter I had a sick shameful feeling, I saw again her smiling eyes and kind sad face and I hated myself. I resolved to be more generous in future and to refuse to court popularity by joining in the teacher-knocking banter. But of course, I could not stick to my resolution, the pressure was too great when Miss Moy-Evans, our little grey-haired English teacher confided in me that she believed in fairies!

Poor unmarried disappointed teachers of the 1940s, their sweethearts lost in the Great War, the generation of surplus women, why couldn't we have been nicer to them? Why did we despise them just because they were unmarried? Why were our mothers considered more successful just because they had 'caught' a man, any man? We girls had swallowed whole the prevailing belief that to be complete a woman had to have a man, and we carried that belief with us into adulthood.

LEARNING ABOUT WOMEN *Mary*

Would there have been a place called the Hen House with an event called 'Growing Old Disgracefully' without the Women's Movement? The answer must be No! How did the Women's Movement enter into my own life and how important was it – and is it?

First there was the Housewives Register. We met, the first three or four members of the York group (I suppose it must have been in 1961) in Betty's Café! What a wonderful experience our meetings were. For the first time I realised what good company a group of women can be. I'd often felt at a disadvantage as a woman growing up – never being expected to take the initiative, always the passive partner, the second best. But here we were enjoying each other's company and organising what happened at our meetings for ourselves.

We talked about the European Common Market once, I remember. It was just beginning to be talked about then. We went on a Peace March through the City with our pushchairs to protest about irradiated milk. We read books like Virginia Woolf's *Orlando*.

The ideas of the Women's Movement came later. I went through all my mature student days without coming across them – even though one of my degree subjects was sociology. Women featured in sociology in those days only as *problems* – as single parents, being poor, as working mothers, as widows – never as agents or subjects in their own right. When we first heard about a book called *The Sociology of Housework*, it sounded ridiculous.

I'd taken for granted 'bitch' and 'cow' and such words, for women; the universal 'he' of *man*kind in history; the exclusion of women for centuries from public life, the professions, the franchise, education. Then I met younger women colleagues and the world began to change. It was they who opened my eyes to the possibility of teaching my own subjects of sociology, psychology etc differently. Was it true for instance, that women, by virtue of their *nature*, make good mothers and must be the ones to do all the nurturing and servicing? I began to look back at my own life anew and to understand better what it means to be a woman in a patriarchal society. I joined Women's Groups, a consciousness-raising group and read many of the early classics of the Women's Movement. It was a new beginning to my life. That was in the 1970s and 1980s. But what does the Women's Movement mean to me now that I'm 68, retired, living on my own in the 1990s and with no end to the Recession in sight?

I'm finding it very depressing to think of the state of the world and its future – except for the Women's Movement. I do not think in terms of 'post-feminism' – ever! It is the vocabulary of the Women's Movement which provides the women of my generation with the means to redefine old age for ourselves and in our terms. Ageism is an oppression just as racism and sexism are, or the oppression of one social class by another. It is from the Women's Movement that women like myself draw our strength and inspiration to fight all these oppressions. I still – almost – believe it is a movement to change the world!

There is a change coming I think in the lives of girls and women. Yes. But it is up to us to make it come.
                                                    Alice Munro

CHAPTER THREE

To the Hen House

Our autobiographies closed as each of us reached a critical turning point in our lives when we were looking for new directions. Our searches led us as individuals to the Hen House for a course called 'Growing Old Disgracefully' from which we emerged with a network of friends and a desire to spread our enthusiasm.

By describing some of what happened on the course we are hoping to inspire you to try out some new activities you never thought you could do, or to re-sharpen some skills that have lain dormant. We recognise that not all people can go on a course but any of the activities can be done elsewhere. We recommend these as group activities because a group generates contagious energy, and its members provide impetus, encouragement and acceptance for each other.

Bear in mind that each of us said 'I can't do that, I don't know how' at some time during the five days we spent together. Then we tried anyway and were surprised when we actually enjoyed participating. We were not half pleased either when our painting or music-making or dancing turned out better than expected. But it was the process rather than the product that provided most of the satisfaction.

At the course there were 22 women ranging in age from mid-fifties to mid-seventies. Unfortunately there were no women of colour. Also, everyone there had sufficient means to pay the fees and travel costs so we obviously were not a representative sample of all ageing women. There was enough diversity in our backgrounds, however, to make the sharing of our different life experiences enriching for us all.

Because we came together as strangers, we had no preconceived expectations of each other. For some it was the first time ever to form relationships based solely on one's own personhood, free from the identification of wife, partner, mother, daughter, employee. In retrospect we realise that bringing that many women together without spouses, children, lovers or bosses is a radical act, no matter what the activities. By the end of the session we had started to use our own voices, free from fear of judgement or censure. Perhaps that is the crux of growing old disgracefully: you disentangle yourself from the identity and opinions of others and finally start being who you want to be.

Group Activities

We generated our activities according to the skills and interests of the members. No cliques or hierarchies developed; each woman contributed whatever expertise she could and each participated whenever she wanted, with no pressure to perform to anyone else's standards. We sang, danced, drummed, painted, exercised, talked, ate, took walks, made life-story collages, played childhood games, shared our accomplishments, discovered feelings we thought we had successfully stowed away, and explored topics ranging from assertiveness to sexuality to stereotypes of old women. And we spent a lot of time laughing, not at each other but with each other. We discovered that the inner child who loves to play and learn is alive and well in each of us, and that age in and of itself is no barrier to fun and excitement.

Making Music

One person brought a variety of simple rhythm instruments – drums, rattles, castanets, bells and the like – and she started us out with a basic beat, as Anne describes here:

> Sitting, legs wide apart, with an African drum between my knees. Ten women holding different instruments. Tom-tom-TOM, stress on the last beat, tom-tom-TOM repeated again and again without rest, without a break. Arms aching, mind in a trance-like state, picking up the rhythms of the others, fitting them into a complete tapestry. We sit drumming, we make music, we move as one in our creativity.

Afterwards we played back the tape-recording of the session and everyone was amazed that we actually sounded good! Did we say we couldn't drum?

If you can get hold of some percussion instruments, try getting a group together for a drumming session. But if not, try drumming along with some music, using tins, spoons, jars, tables or anything to hand. It might not sound very musical but it's wonderfully liberating!

Assertiveness

In some of our sessions we learned new techniques for growing old disgracefully, for instance we practised being more assertive and setting boundaries, a skill Barbara was able to put into practice with her noisy neighbours when she returned home:

> The workshop on assertiveness had been fun and we all enjoyed role-playing situations in which we had found it hard to be assertive. I left the course determined to put the ideas into practice and ran through them in my head as I drove home. DERS – D for describing the situation, E for expressing how it made you feel, R for stating your request and S for a suggested compromise. This was the cool, rational approach to potentially confrontational situations.

I often go to bed late and look forward to a pleasant lie-in the next morning. But on Saturday morning what was that ungodly noise at 6.45am? The twins next door were practising on their recorders in the room which shared a wall with mine. To say that they were not very good players would be over-praising them. They were awful in duplicate! And this early morning practice became a regular torture. One week-end my patience ran out. 'Right,' I thought, 'this is a chance to put my assertiveness to the test.'

At a decent hour I stood on the next-door front step, nervously rehearsing my **DERS** routine. My neighbour opened the door: she did not look very friendly – perhaps she resented being woken at 6.45 herself? I said, 'Can you spare a minute?' She didn't ask me in but stood waiting. OK – **D** for Describe the situation.

'Your girls started playing their recorders at 6.45 this morning and it woke me up,' I Described. 'This is very early to start making such a noise and I don't like being woken up so early,' I Expressed. 'I would like you to ask them not to start so early,' I Requested. 'Could they wait until after 8.00 or perhaps go downstairs to practise?' I Suggested as a compromise.

'They practice when they feel like it and I am certainly not going to stop them,' she said, shutting the door firmly in my face. Defeat of assertive woman.

But this story has a happy ending because, for whatever reason, the twins never again played their recorders so early in the morning, so maybe my assertiveness did work after all.

Being assertive does not mean being aggressive but standing up for your own rights. Assertiveness is a skill that needs practice and this is where role-playing comes in useful. Think of some situations which have left you feeling that you should have acted or spoken up, then act them out in a group. It is useful to change roles, switching from playing the assertive character to the one on the receiving end. This can give an insight to the motivation of the offender, for instance the addictive smoker who annoys people at the next table in a restaurant or a young person who refuses to give up a seat to an older one. Role-playing is not only helpful and instructive but also great fun.

Painting

At one of the sessions we painted and then combined our works to produce amazingly coherent composites, showing once again that creativity gains added dimensions when individuals link with each other. No-one felt like an accomplished artist on her own but together our results were astounding. Shirley tells of her disgracefulness as she joined in:

> Pencils and paints and crayons and water. I hadn't dipped a paintbrush in a paintbox since I was at primary school. The orange was vibrant and the yellow pure. I mixed the two together. Muddy colour. Oh dear, try again.
>
> I was attempting to paint a sky. A wide semicircle of glowing sun appeared. I was a child again, getting wet and dirty but with no stern teacher standing over me telling me I couldn't put those two colours together or that I was naughty for making a mess.
>
> I splashed here, drew a line there. I experimented with small strokes and then with wild abandon. My page quickly filled with the radiant heat of the sun, the like of which might suit a tropical paradise. It was wild and wonderful.
>
> Other people were painting their versions of foregrounds and backgrounds, forests, animals, skylines and playgrounds. We put them together into one painting. Magic!

Many women have such little confidence in their artistic ability that they would feel inadequate in an organised art class. But there is nothing to stop a group of women from clubbing together to buy some art materials – paper, paint, brushes and felt pens – and putting aside a set time, a morning or a day a week, to enjoy the pleasure of creativity. There will be nobody judging whether you have done 'well' or created a 'good' painting, you can just enjoy yourself and as an added bonus you might well find that, while your hands are busy, the conversation flows.

Paper Collage

Another activity suggested by one of the women on the course was to make a paper collage that represented something about your life, using coloured paper and glue but no scissors. Edith describes how discussing the meaning of her collage became almost a therapeutic exercise:

> We were sitting on the floor listening to each person explain her collage. Here was Virginia's, a small white dot on a solid background, and her moving explanation about it being a projection of her near-death experience some years ago; she recounted it almost as though she was repeating the experience. When it was my turn I wondered how it would be possible for me to analyse the collage I had just completed. It was just some haphazardly torn pieces of coloured paper pasted together, creating an interesting relationship between the different shapes and colours, all very satisfying. I looked again at the arrangement of shapes placed at various angles to each other, at the slanted rolled up piece of paper pasted across them. I was about to say 'It's just a pleasing design' but instead I heard myself explaining 'The boxes convey the way my life is locked into neat little compartments and the roll of paper is me all tied up under tension, unable to decide how to carry on.' I was utterly amazed by this explanation, it just tumbled out without me being aware of what I was saying.

Writing

We found that the writing sessions led to some of our richest experiences at the Hen House. One of the techniques we used was to choose a particular period in our lives, to give ourselves time to focus on a memory from that time and then to write about it. Our group chose to write about the Second World War as a momentous experience we had all lived through at an important formative time in our lives.

We sat around the room letting our minds move back in time. Many of us had no confidence in our writing ability but we split up and went off to find quiet corners where we could write. When we re-gathered half an hour later everybody had written something and, as we went round the room reading aloud what we had written, the atmosphere became electric. The stories came alive, they evoked with clarity the feelings, the fears and the excitement of being a child or a young woman in wartime. (Barbara)

Many of us had described our memories of the day war was declared, the mixture of confusion and excitement, of something dramatic which would change our lives. Myfanwy Fitzgerald described listening to Chamberlain's broadcast:

I was twelve years old and I knew Neville Chamberlain's voice. I knew everyone was waiting to hear if we were at war with Germany but I felt that it really wasn't anything to do with me. After the historic announcement someone switched off the wireless. There was a stunned silence – all but for the ebony clock ticking away ... At one o'clock the siren sounded and because we were lost and unsure we all went back to Granny's because she knew what to do, we just sat down and ate our roast beef and Yorkshire pudding.

Others described their experience of bombing, of gas-masks and air-raid shelters. Irene Smithe remembered her father coming home shaking with tears:

I had never seen a man cry and the shock was awful. Across the road was an infants' school and he had been looking at the five year olds lining up in the playground, trying on their gas-masks. So this was what war meant.

Barbara remembered daylight raids before the school shelters were completed:

When the siren sounded we were all sent home, running through the street with our gas-masks in their boxes flip-flapping as we ran. The road seemed endless, the hill too steep. The planes were overhead – ours or theirs? ... Night after night the sirens sounded their eerie wailing and I would be lifted from my warm bed and rushed down to the shelter. One night the crashing, crumping sounds were so close that the ground shook and the next morning as we crept out of the shelter, stretching our cramped limbs, we found that where the house two doors away had stood was nothing but a smoking ruin.

Shirley had vivid memories of rationing and the patient queueing for anything a bit special such as the occasional orange:

We had four ration books, bread, flour, meat, chocolate, eggs, they were all rationed. I remember my Dad's Sunday ritual of dividing the two-ounce bar of chocolate, the family ration per week. After lunch he would go to the cupboard, unwrap the paper ceremoniously and delicately break the eight squares, trying not to make any crumbs, and give us two squares each.

I remember one shop in our High Street having a delivery of oranges. The queue went down the hill to the bottom and as we slowly climbed the hill my Mum and I wondered if the supplies would last until we reached the top. It must have taken three hours and the chatter and excitement rose as we got nearer. We feared the sirens going off which would mean losing our place in the queue. We enviously watched people leaving the shop clutching their purchases. When we got to the head of the queue, glory be, they were on the last crate. We had four ration books so we got four oranges, rather small but bright, with a strong smell which I had forgotten. I was only nine. We were worn out with queuing but didn't complain as we carried our prize home. I handled my orange long before eating it, stroking it and smelling it. It was almost tragic to peel it. But I drank every drop of the juice of that orange, the taste of which has never been equalled.

None of us would have believed that our memories were of consequence to anyone else or that we could write well enough to affect others. How wrong we were. The power of reviving memories and sharing them is profound. Truth and emotion transcend any lack of skill in writing; when you say things that are true and important to you, the passion comes through and the feelings are identifiable. There is so much to be gained by sharing thoughts and memories and valuing each other's stories, and it works every time. Try it with three or four friends, choose a focal point, for instance the year you were 12, 14 or 15, the year you left home or the day the war ended; give yourselves time to think then go off and write for 30 minutes. The limited time is a marvellous spur to honest and spontaneous writing. Then share your writing by reading it aloud to the group. This is the best part and never fails to be entertaining and moving – be prepared for laughter and tears.

We suggest shared memories as an example of a group activity which can get you into writing. But too much looking back can be a self-indulgence, drawing energy from the vital process of growing old disgracefully. Once a writing group is well established the focus can be shifted to the present and the future and then the sharing of ideas can be exciting and provocative, leading into new and previously undreamed-of fields.

Talking about Sexuality

There are some subjects you might want to discuss but not write about. In our group we found that all 22 of us wanted a workshop on sexuality although we agreed that it was a very difficult subject for women of our age to discuss openly. Everyone wanted to take part yet no one wanted to be the first to speak, as Anne describes:

> The workshop on sexuality started tentatively. The facilitator suggested breaking into small groups but no-one wanted to do that – nobody wanted to miss anything that others might say!
>
> What a difficult subject for a group of older women who

had been told all their lives that sex and sexuality were taboo topics. We shifted uncomfortably in our seats, coughed discreetly, avoided eye contact, or looked at each other expectantly. What would we hear? What would we say?

A bluebottle buzzed. Someone offered a quotation from Jung, a few theories, then a long silence. I felt that I had a contribution to make, but no, I did not feel safe enough to say anything. Someone talked of the pleasures of touch; it seemed a risky subject and was barely taken up by the others. Another long silence. I was beginning to wonder whether this workshop would ever get off the ground.

The voice of a much older woman broke the silence as she quietly said that she would like to share her experience with the group. We were all moved as she spoke about the difficulty of intercourse with her elderly frail husband, about the pleasure they enjoyed, lying side-by-side, touching and holding one another. She told us how she missed that loving

closeness now that he had died. I felt that she was very brave to talk about such intimate matters in a group. I was glad she had broken the silence.

Others without husbands or lovers – single, widowed or divorced – expressed sadness at their need for intimacy with men and the little likelihood that they would find it again at this time of their lives. Someone suggested that there might be other options. Could I trust myself to be open about my feelings for women? If I spoke out would the rest of the group shun me? feel threatened? revile me? At last I plucked up my courage and talked about an alternative way of giving and receiving pleasure in a Lesbian relationship. I said it quietly and waited for the ground to open beneath my feet. After an expectant pause I heard another voice telling the group that she was still married but she had loved women and enjoyed intimate relationships with them.

The outcome of this seemingly so-risky pronouncement was just the opposite of what I had expected. Other women showed interest and respect for my openness. I was thanked by the woman who spoke after me for thus allowing her to express her feelings.

This was the first time I had 'come out' except to close friends and family. I felt it to be an important step forward in my personal development, in my openness and on my path to growing old disgracefully.

So many issues were raised in this workshop and in our subsequent discussions that we realised how fundamental the subject of sexuality and body image is to women's feelings about themselves. In Chapter 5 you will find a selection of the writings which resulted from these discussions.

Play-time

Not everyone at the Hen House course attended or participated in every workshop. At Anne's 'Afternoon at Mablethorpe' four women allowed themselves to be children at play:

We were planning the programme and people were offering

to lead groups on various mysterious and prestigious subjects. Being normally a fairly quiet and diffident member of any group, more a follower than a leader, I surprised myself when I volunteered to lead a group, an offer for which I had no skills or experience. I was delighted when three women decided to chance their luck and join me on a nearby beach for a session on remembered childhood games. So we drove to Mablethorpe, a most uninspiring seaside town, on the edge of flat, uninspiring countryside, which seemed to consist wholly of a grey-looking holiday camp, grey shacks for shops and a few grey people. The beach itself was deserted and extended for what looked like miles, over sand-dunes and unusual coastal plants, to the far distant sea-shore.

We hollowed out comfortable places for ourselves in the sand dunes on this warm sunny day and sat in our small circle. We knew nothing of one another except our names. We allowed ourselves to go back in time and memory to our childhoods, to try to recall and relive the games which had been important parts of our lives. Edith, from New York, told us about the street games she had played with her friends in the Bronx. Her eyes sparkled, she was once again the child playing Red-Rover, Stoop-ball, Jacks and Potsie, she relived each one in turn. Inevitably her thoughts strayed to other aspects of her childhood – her parents, the streets, the Depression, other children, the similarities and differences between games in the US and in England. Shirley was transported back to North London, feeling, remembering, associating, being a child playing hopscotch, building sand-castles, skipping. This happened too for Marguerite and for me, until we were all shouting, singing, demonstrating the games – What's the time Mr Wolf? Grandmother's Footsteps – which became so real and so immediate.

Then four little girls kicked off their shoes and started walking, running, skipping, hopping towards the sea. They trod on each other's shadows, jumped in little pools of water and threw stones to make them bounce across the sea. They paddled and got their skirts and trousers wet before they reluctantly dragged themselves away from these delights for an ice-cream and a return to adulthood.

I had planted the seed of the idea and facilitated its being and I felt grateful to the others for having trust in my idea and sharing themselves with me.

Childhood games open a rich vein of memory for most of us and, once you start thinking about them, you are sure to find that the memories evoke the streets or fields of your childhood with vivid clarity. Sharing these games within a group releases other long-buried memories and helps to re-awaken the children within yourselves.

The Beginning of the Rest of Our Lives

By the end of the Hen House course lives had been changed, and 22 ageing women left feeling that we had made wonderful new friends with whom to laugh and to cry. This is how Barbara describes it:

> Arriving at the Hen House at a meal-time, I looked around the dining room and thought 'What am I doing here with all these old women?' Five days later, as we hugged and said our farewells I knew that there were at least five of these women who would be my friends for years to come. What brought about this metamorphosis was the sharing of experiences, memories, pain and sadness and, above all, of joy and laughter. I think it is the laughter I remember most, the fun of it all. It is hard to recall exactly what was so funny but, in a way, like children we became so in touch with our own feelings that both laughter and tears were never very far from the surface. The party on the last night was a free-ranging joyous event where we danced and sang and played statues, savouring the sense of release we had gained by letting down the barriers and finding the children we had buried within ourselves.

In the end we all had a better sense of what it might mean to grow old disgracefully, but let's save that for the next chapter. This one closes with a poem by Irene Smithe. Irene was at the Hen House at the same time as we were and, as well as this poem, sent us several pieces which we felt must be included in this book.

NOT THE HEN HOUSE

The yakkety-yak and the laughter
Is not the clucking of hens,
But the turning of keys in locks
The withdrawal of bolts
Experience freed,
The coming together of souls.

The yeast is fermenting now
Leavening our tomorrows,
And safe in the lives of women
The wine will be slowly maturing.

CHAPTER FOUR

Growing Old Disgracefully

If you look up 'disgraceful' in a dictionary, the definition may include such words as scandalous, dishonourable, shameful. Perhaps that is why, whenever we mention the title of this book, we bring smiles to people's faces. They probably picture an older woman letting go and making a fool of herself.

That's not what we mean at all. We would like to offer you a very different interpretation. We use 'growing old disgracefully' as a challenge to the image of 'growing old gracefully', which implies that we are to be silent, invisible, compliant and selflessly available for the needs of others. In other words, to age gracefully is to continue to be the passive, obedient, unobtrusively good girls we were socialised to be. Well, we're not prepared to do that; we're going to make up for lost time.

Like many women of our generation, the conditions of our lives have dictated that we repress our own dreams and desires in order to tend to everyone else's. Our demanding jobs both inside and outside the home have often left us with precious little time, money or energy for self-nurturing. Having now reached a time in life when our web of family and work obligations is shrinking, we can seize the opportunity to actualise what we were only able to dream during years of self-denial. We discover that there is time left to connect to ourselves, to say 'It's my turn now' and to find out who and what we mean.

It is a challenging task to identify one's true feelings and wishes after a lifetime of denying them or deferring to the needs of others. Women over 60 learned how to be 'good girls' before the current wave of feminism, before the age of pop psychology and the language of co-dependency, before the 'do-your-own-thing' philosophy, and before an increasing life-span and adequate income gave women the possibility of being active and independent in their old age. It would be tempting but useless to sit around and whine about being cheated, so some of us are opting for growing old disgracefully instead. We may have missed our turn before but we intend to have it now. Our heap of discarded dreams is shrinking as we pursue delayed interests or new life-styles, defying the stereotypes of older women which do injustice to our skills, resourcefulness, enthusiasm, curiosity and diversity.

This is not to deny that there are still very real objective limitations for women. Issues of economics, health and social pressures cannot be wished away. Ageism, sexism, racism and other forms of institutional oppressions will still exist as barriers and will only be overcome by concerted co-operative efforts. Not the least limiting are the internalised shoulds and oughts which restrict and confine us. Ageing, though, holds out the possibility, like no other time in life, for finally saying, as the American cartoonist William Steig did in the 1950s, 'Public opinion no longer interests me.' Perhaps the stories about people becoming cantankerous in their old age are really about how they no longer hide their true feelings behind a façade of polite respectability.

How to Begin Growing Old Disgracefully

For some, release from social expectations is a frightening prospect, but for those ready to take the risks there is an infinite number of ways to begin. Even very small steps can be empowering. One woman in our original group at the Hen House said that she began by no longer volunteering to do all the flower arrangements for her church; another stopped going to church altogether. Irene Smithe sent us her personal guidelines for growing old disgracefully:

(a) Being as assertive as my nature allows

(b) not being put off by others' opinions and having confidence in my own

(c) making the effort to do something creative but, on the other hand, not feeling too bad about myself if I am tempted to collapse in front of the TV

(d) conquering irrational fears, eg of travelling alone in unfamiliar places, or of suddenly feeling too ill to carry on

(e) saying to myself 'just do it' and finding it's not too hard

(f) at the same time as all this, concentrating on enjoyment, the operative syllable being 'joy'; realising that this doesn't have to mean some great transcendental experience but can come from the minor pleasures of life. Most of the major pleasures are ruled out by my circumstances (including too little money and a few physical problems) but there are many more minor ones than I had expected.

There are no universal recipes or prescriptions, for what is a challenge to one woman may appear perfectly safe, even mundane, to another. You might find a simple change, such as cooking something that *you* especially like instead of what the family expects, may be enough of a first step. Each time you assert yourself and the sky remains where it is instead of falling on your head, you gain a bit more courage for the next breakthrough.

Growing old disgracefully may not be for everyone. Many women do not feel the necessity for change at this stage of their lives, particularly those within loving relationships who are looking forward to having more time with their partners. However, even these women may find themselves unexpectedly constricted when their partners retire and are home all day. And there is a large and growing population of older women who, due to widowhood or divorce, face life alone perhaps for the first time. Often these are women who have lived their lives caring for others: their husbands, children, grandchildren, aged relatives, work colleagues and so on. Now they are at a point when they need to say, 'What do *I* want to do with the rest of my life? What do I want to be when I grow up?' It's not easy to find an answer alone but in old or new networks and friendships, alongside other women who are asking the same questions, the search can be a joyful process.

In the Company of Others

In our own group it has been an unexpected but welcome revelation to us that close attachments and new friendship networks can be created at this stage of life. Our common commitment to changing old rules and patterns has nourished our connection and facilitated our growth. Although we each could have taken steps on our own, we have found that the others have provided the encouragement necessary to keep up our resolve. We are a safety net for one another as we try to break the patterns of behaviour imposed on us by family, friends and social institutions. We still care about and see our old friends with whom we have shared so much, but we value the life-affirming support and love of our new circle as well. We intend to grow old disgracefully together!

A useful exercise you can try for yourself is to take a large sheet of paper and coloured pencils and draw a dot in the middle to represent yourself. Then using different colours you begin to draw the networks which connect you to others. Some need to be very close to you at the centre, perhaps your partner, children, siblings or parents. Then bit by bit the sheet becomes covered with the lines of connectedness. These networks seem to be essential to the lives of women, they give strength and substance. A life which stopped short at the inner circle of close family would be lacking the richness which can be gained from the wider networks of friendships and shared interests.

If our minds and hearts are open, each new experience adds more friends and networks. Shared interests, shared work, shared holidays, all lay the foundations for friendships which can enrich your life. But women know that friendship is a two-way process and does not develop by accident. Within marriage it is common for the wife to maintain the friendships and create the social fabric of their joint lives. Men more often have friends with whom they play golf or go for a drink but this is very different from the qualities women give and expect from friendship. It is no wonder that women are more able to cope with life alone after a divorce, while men usually lose no time in finding another woman to nurture them.

Women have always known the strength they can give each other and have often drawn together to use this strength in subversive ways. For example the repressed Amish women, denied pleasures and adornment by the strictures of their religion, nevertheless stitched their joy and love of beauty into the patchwork quilts which they created as a shared activity.

There are many networks of older women already established and some of them are listed at the end of this book. You can form your own through women you meet at classes, workshops, activities and the like. Some of us are getting together in local Growing Old Disgracefully groups in different parts of the country and we would welcome your participation. See the Resources Guide on page 221 for ways to contact someone in your area.

It's Your Turn Now

For those ready to risk it, growing old disgracefully means giving yourself the chance to explore exciting possibilities at any age. It is not about trying to stay young for ever or judging yourself by the Joan Collins image that the slick magazines love to exploit. It means that you are free to create your own models for who you are and who you want to become, that you will give yourself permission to try new experiences or revive old ambitions and to age with a sense of self-esteem and playfulness. It is an acknowledgement of the creative, impulsive, spontaneous child-like parts of the self.

Growing Old Disgracefully is also a commitment. It's not a hobby you take up, like dried-flower arranging or stamp collecting; it is a way of life that grows from the contradictions in women's experiences, from the antagonism between our curious and life-affirming core and our socialisation as women. It grows from every small subversive act and every strategy we've used to help us survive. It is already there in those rare moments when, like weeds poking through cracks in concrete, we give the world a glimpse of an authentic person who refuses to play by all the patriarchal rules. It is there, just waiting to be released.

In the selection of our written pieces beginning on page 118 we elaborate on our individual definitions for growing old disgracefully, and tell some of the ways in which we are putting them into practice. We write about our old and new attitudes and behaviours, others' reactions to them, and the importance of our supportive friendships and networks. The themes we have woven together form a patchwork, not unlike the non-linear web of women's lives.

Just before we get to those, however, we want to share with you some ideas for exercises and games which we have found helpful and often hilarious. They can be adapted to your particular circumstances or act as a catalyst for you to create your own. However you use them, we hope you have as much fun with them as we have.

GAMES

As positive as we feel about our need to grow old disgracefully, it can be quite hard to know where to start. You need a little encouragement to break with those habits of a lifetime which restrain you. We talk elsewhere about how to set up the sort of support groups in which such things can happen but here are some ways we've found of making such groups work well.

Firstly, you need to build up trust between members of the group and we've found that a variety of games can help. They are not the sort of games which children play, but they can help release those childish feelings within you that may have been submerged by responsibilities and life experiences.

Breaking the Ice

It's not easy to relax with a group of strangers, even if you have the shared focus of growing old disgracefully. So we recommend that you start by introducing yourself to one other person in the group for, say, 5–10 minutes. Then let the other person tell you about themselves. This done, you rejoin the larger group and introduce your partner to everyone else. So do all the other partners. It may not seem much like a game but there can be a lot of fun in noticing what is remembered in your re-telling and what mistakes need to be corrected. It's not an exam but a lovely and enjoyable way to concentrate on each other and learn, often with delight and surprise about the parallels and diversity of other women's lives.

Of course, the first round of introductions may only be relatively superficial but you will find it an effective way of beginning that important trust-building that will grow as you begin to shed some of those protective onion skins that mask the woman beneath, eager for fun and friendship.

All the games we have played have helped relieve tension and liberated us to be more honest about our feelings, releasing us from often debilitating and inhibiting self-consciousness. It may depend on your mood, or how many risks you are prepared to take with language or self-revelations. Our experience is that the more we have grown to know, respect and love each other, the more fun we have had with the games.

Song Time

One sort of game – with infinite possible variations – is what we call Song Time. Here is what Barbara wrote about what it does for her.

> I'm no great singer. I can hear the tune inside my head but very often what comes out of my mouth bears very little relation to it. This makes me sad because I love singing and it gives me real pleasure to open up and let the music flow. I have really enjoyed one of the games we play because it allows me to do just that. We choose a theme and each in turn thinks of a song which relates to it or even just includes a reference to it. You start to sing and then everybody joins in. Nobody is ever out. If you can't think of a song, the turn passes to the next person and you can rejoin on the next round. For instance, we chose the theme Heavenly Bodies. Our songs ranged from 'Blue Moon', 'Moon River', 'Paper Moon', to 'Twinkle Twinkle Little Star' and 'The Sun Has Got His Hat On'. We dredged up songs our mothers sang, some of them pre-First World War, nursery rhymes, folk songs, rock and roll, blues, schmaltzy songs of the 1930s, war-time ballads ... we were amazed by the sheer size of our repertoire.
>
> The joy of this game in a group of women of similar ages is the lovely flash of recognition when somebody sings a song which was part of your own youth or childhood. It becomes more than just a game, but another step in recalling the past and sharing your memories.

There are numerous themes you can choose and you will surprise yourself at the songs you can dredge up from your memory and also the way it can both relax you and draw you closer to others. Some of the themes we have used are the names of flowers, colours, birds, body parts, places and so on.

Story Telling

Edith's favourite game is Story Telling, but one word at a time. She remembers her first session in our group.

The story telling was starting on its round again. We were permitted one word at each turn, when we could also decide where the punctuation should go. I was feeling tired that evening after a full day of talking and writing and, as I hadn't played the game before, I felt I would rather be in bed with a book. However, I allowed myself to be persuaded to stay and join the fun. Fun it certainly was, dissolving into side-holding laughter. All the tensions that had built up in the course of the day evaporated. What could be so funny about a simple word game? Have you ever tried to tell a story word by a single word?

Frequently, favourite words began to appear and my special one that evening was *dzo*, a word I had never come across until it was trotted out the previous evening at a Scrabble session. With its first use I preferred the recently acquired definition – 'a dzo is a Tibetan goat'. 'What use is a demented ghost?' asked Mary who hadn't heard clearly. That almost brought the roof down! So whenever I was stuck for a word to continue the narrative, out would come dzo, full stop. Another re-appearing word was *protuberance* which was worked into the story in some pretty strange ways. We actually were forced to stop the game eventually when we all collapsed from laughter – too exhausted to carry on. The built-up stress of the day had quietly disappeared.

Limericks

Another of the many other games we've tried and which we've found particularly good at breaking through blocks in our writing is to each write a limerick. This has also been useful when we've been bereft of ideas, stuck in a difficult mood or just in need of some laughter.

Here Edith explains how writing limericks helped us on one such occasion.

Our spirits were flagging, our energies too; we had spent a busy afternoon letting the child in us loose, entering into the spirit of having our photographs taken on the apparatus in a wonderful local children's playground. We had jumped rope, climbed onto a rope bridge, stretched out on a slide, and balanced on a see-saw. It had been great fun but a writing session had been pencilled in for the afternoon and the words weren't flowing. The usually reviving cup of tea had not worked. Revitalisation hadn't been effected. More desultory talk followed, then someone suggested trying our hand at limericks, a sort of limbering-up mental exercise. We were slow starting but, when the half-hour limit had been reached, everyone begged for more time. The outcome was productive with some very bright five-liners.

The challenge to rhyme always attracts and the very simplicity of the device spurs you on. Both Edward Lear and The Reverend Dodgson (Lewis Carroll) concocted some memorable limericks and are well worth a read. It's advisable not to aspire to the complicated rhymes of Cole Porter or Ogden Nash at the outset. A limerick is a five-line verse, the first, second and fifth lines rhyming, with equivalent metres; the third and fourth lines with a different rhyme.

Try it, you'll be surprised at what you can do. It doesn't matter how crude or unpolished your limerick may be; that's what often produces the most laughter.

On the next page are some of our limericks.

One old woman said to another
'Why blame everything on your mother?
Can't you discern
That she, in her turn,
Learned her mothering from your grandmother?'

Six disgraceful old women are we!
We're disgraceful as women can be.
We hug and we sing
And we dance in a ring –
Come and join us at our Hen Party!

In a manner of speaking, they say
Old women should sit and go grey.
But the book of our lives
Says we're other than wives
And can live to the full every day.

Making a Web

Barbara describes another game.

You will need as many odd balls of wool as you have members of the group, the brighter and more varied the colours the better. Each woman has a ball of wool which she ties loosely around her waist. Throw your ball to any other woman, totally at random. As you catch a ball, pass it round your waist and throw it to somebody else. The process is great fun in itself but what is remarkable is watching the web develop. Once you have used all your wool, you can pass your loop down and step out of it, then form a circle pulling the web taut between you. It is hard to believe but the web is strong enough to hold the weight of a woman and, as each in turn trusts the rest of the group to take her weight, warm and joyful feelings are generated. We found it impossible to dispose of our web when we tried this activity, so we pegged it out on the grass and left it there.

Adjectives

What does being disgraceful mean to you? That's the question we are trying to answer for ourselves in this book. However, we got bogged down sometimes and found that playing the following game helped us to get to the crux of our understanding. Any number of people can play. Each person, in turn, contributes an adjective to describe what it is you are trying to understand. We've found that it's more fun doing it alphabetically. Don't spend too much time thinking out your word. The faster you go, the funnier it can be. The first time we played it started with a round of what it means to be old and disgraceful, and came up with adjectives like *active, bouncy, changing, dancing*. Sometimes we cheated when it came to the Xs, with words like *Xentric!* Then we did another round describing what it did *not* mean for us to grow old disgracefully – and that brought forth words like *aggressive, bossy, compliant, disagreeable*, and so on. Have a go and see what you come up with.

But don't stop there. Try other games. Invent your own! And see what a release it can be.

People only grow old by deserting their ideals. Years may wrinkle the skin, but to give up interests wrinkles the soul.   Joy, age 68, Hen House participant

Age is something that doesn't matter, unless you are a cheese.   Billie Burke

INSATIABLE CURIOSITY *Maxine*

Many years ago I read an article by a woman in her forties who claimed that she had come to terms with ageing. She was growing old gracefully, which included, for her, letting go of many of her fantasies and being content with wonderful memories. As an example, she said she had made peace with the reality that she would never fulfil her dream of standing on a balcony overlooking the French Riviera, sipping champagne with a new lover.

At the time I thought she was a model of sensibility. Now I want to ask her 'Why not?' True, by virtue of class differences, most of us will never see the French Riviera, with or without a lover, but it doesn't seem a dream that should be tossed on to the dust heap by virtue of age alone. If growing old gracefully means not aiming for one's craziest dreams then I want no part of it. Even if I end up sipping warm milk instead of champagne, overlooking a local river instead of the Riviera, the dream, including the new lover, sounds perfectly reasonable to me.

Anyone who is still curious about the world could never be content to grow old gracefully. I remember the story by Kipling in which a young animal's insatiable curiosity led him into dangerous situations, brought him spankings and disapproval, but ultimately turned him into a new and improved version of an elephant, complete with trunk. I identify with that story. While I haven't grown a trunk (yet), my back sprouts a pack now and again; and though my insatiable curiosity has landed me in more tight spots than I care to remember, it has also propelled me into untold, unanticipated delights. Curiosity may yet kill this old cat, but at least I will have had some great adventures along the way.

LOOKING IN THE MIRROR *Anne*

I've just had a swim, then a spell sitting in the sun. I feel full of energy and strength. My skin is glowing, my step is light. Pink trousers, shocking pink T-shirt. Short fair hair blowing in the breeze, softly tickling my forehead.

I feel I could walk 20 miles, dance all day, hum, sing, play childish games. I feel light-headed, without a care in the world.

There is nothing I could not do if I wanted. Travel alone, write a poem, weave a tapestry, paint a picture.

My inner feeling is one of joy, contentment, peace with myself and the world outside me. My inner eye conjures up this tall, brown, supple, energetic creature, exuding good health and enjoyment from every pore, eyes sparkling, feet hardly touching the ground.

Home again, I pass the mirror.

Who is this person who has just come in with me? I didn't invite her in; she just came; she just followed me in! She's medium height, face reddened by the sun, skin heavy around the jaw and chin. She walks with a slightly clumsy gait as she drops her swim-things to the floor. She gazes short-sightedly into my mirror at her hair, greying at the temples.

Then she sees past the reddened skin and heavy jowls. She sees past the clumsy body, greying hair.

She sees me – a tall, brown, supple energetic creature, healthy and happy, and I know I can accept this stranger in my home, and in my soul, because she is now so dear and so familiar.

Taking joy in life is a woman's best cosmetic.
Rosalind Russell

GROWING OLD DISGRACEFULLY
Mary

How am I growing old disgracefully? Well, you wouldn't be shocked by my appearance if you met me in the street. And I wouldn't be likely to embarrass you if we stood talking.

For me growing old disgracefully is more an attitude to old age, a defying of the stereotypes, than an outrageous way of behaving. It is a necessary countering of the negative words and images associated with women's ageing: 'old hag', 'old bag', 'old biddy' and so on – ad infinitum!

It is OK for me now, for instance, being an old woman on my own. It's true the world we know best is organised around couples, usually husband and wife, or male and female partners or same-sex partners, but there is a good life to be had as an old woman who is not part of a couple but who is part of a social network which includes a whole range of relationships.

You can test this theory out for yourself. Compare the couples – husbands and wives usually – sitting silent side by side next time you're in a café, with the women in small groups or pairs who are busy talking and listening to each other. Women so engaged used to be accused of gossiping. Remember? Only women gossiped, men *talked* and *discussed*. It is a sign of the strength of the Women's Movement that women's 'gossip' has been reclaimed and revalued. Women know that before the world can be changed we have to talk about it while the men go on killing each other and, very sadly, killing the women and children too.

When we are old there is more time for gossiping. I see old women together arm in arm negotiating a slippery pavement or rough steps. I see them standing with their trolleys gossiping together in the super-market and I rejoice that we have each other, that the

older we grow the more women of our own age there
are around us! We are not going to be identified as 'a
growing social problem', as the social commentators
would have us labelled, but as a thriving, gossiping and
defiant sisterhood.

Yes, there is the fumbling, the constant mislaying of
belongings, the forgetting of the right words and names
but that happened when I was young too! Now I've got
four competent daughters who enjoy putting me right.
Now and again I want to remind them where I've been
and what I've done with my life ... 'Never apologise!
Never make excuses!' I say to myself when this
happens, it only draws attention to the lapse, move on
to the next thing. If *they* still need to prove themselves
I don't. So I relax and resolve to remember the word or
whatever the next time and to have a laugh with my
friends about it when next we meet.

Most of all, growing old disgracefully for me means
that both the free, happy, playful child *and* the wise old
woman are kept alive inside, both together, in my heart
and in my head. This can't just happen; there have to
be opportunities made and taken – joining in the silly
games, or better still starting one off! And the wise old
woman? I think the modern word for wisdom is self-
awareness. And self-awareness, a critical self-awareness,
is best kept alive by listening, by listening and learning
– that will do for a start anyway.

Before I was a feminist, growing old disgracefully
might have meant something quite different – being
shameful, even wicked – at the very least doing things
my mother would have disapproved of! Now it means
being more myself than I've ever been before! And that
feels pretty good – most of the time!

I remember an occasion many years ago when my
sister and I were watching an old fairground organ
playing a waltz. We longed to dance together with the
music but we were surrounded by our children. Their

presence weighed us down. Then suddenly we both stepped into the open space in front of the organ, dancing together. It was a moment none of us has ever forgotten! So daring! So disgraceful! I cherish the memory, it holds the feeling I want to carry with me into my old age.

NEW WAYS *Anne*

Laying foundations for new ways of living,
Finding new ways for receiving and giving,
Time on my own and time spent with others,
Family or friends, colleagues or lovers.

Time used for doing, time just for being,
For touching, for healing, for smelling and seeing.
Time is what matters at this point in life
No longer as daughter or mother or wife.

Time for the me who has slowly emerged
From the embryo creature so often submerged.
Time to expand, to jump and to fly.
To sing and to dance and to laugh and to cry.

To follow the impulse, to act on the feeling,
Skins of the onion are peeling, revealing.
Perhaps to disclose that still core of the soul,
That wisdom and knowledge to make myself whole.

WHAT IT MEANS TO ME TO GROW OLD DISGRACEFULLY *Shirley*

Being 62 is a good age to be. I am comfortable with myself, knowing my limits and able to accept them. I don't have to impress either intellectually or sexually. It is a great delight to be beyond the menstrual cycle with all its anxieties and discomfort. I dismiss the idea of cosmetic surgery for my sagging chins and breasts. The sort of disgracefulness I am proud to acknowledge for myself is the daring to admit to my limitations, but to extend my body and skills as far as I personally wish to go. When my body tells me it has aches and pains, I would like to be able to avoid medication, recognising symptoms of stress and pain, taking such measures as slowing down, analysing the problem, understanding the cause and working it through.

I have two wonderful sons with their loving partners. I have two scrumptious twin grand-daughters for whom I have every reason to live with delight each day. I want to be able to continue to crawl around the floor with them on all fours, roll over, play hide and seek, make silly faces and play the fool without blushing. Who cares who sees me? As long as they and I become friends and enjoy each other's company, that's all that matters.

There was a time though when I was a source of embarrassment to my family. My son Clive could not bear me standing out from the crowd and the phrase 'Mum, Mum' was a family catchword. I remember taking him to public meetings to protest, to support this event or that. If I was moved to speak on the platform, Clive would hold on to my elbow to keep me back. 'Don't', he would beg. If I said 'Let's skip home from school today', or if I laughed loudly and drew attention to us, he would say, 'Mum, Mum, don't.' If I'd give him something exotic or different in his lunch box which might make other children notice, he'd say,

'Mum, Mum, just give me a sandwich like the others.'
If I kissed him or my other son, Bruce, in the street they
would blush and groan, 'Oh Mum, Mum'. All was
embarrassment. If I applauded vigorously or shouted
'Bravo!' at a concert they would reduce themselves
almost to invisibility until they noticed that other
people had followed my example and were also wildly
excited in their own way.

My non-conformity seemed disgraceful in their
terms. But that feeling has changed over the years as I
have become even more disgraceful in my terms.

They were startled but not embarrassed when I told
them I was going to cross America alone by bus. They
were awed when I said I was going to China. Previous
embarrassment had turned into respect. They knew I
would cope and that it was something I needed to do
for myself.

Nowadays they wouldn't be surprised to see me
dancing in the dark, to hear the raucous laughter when
we women get together. Now, it's almost as if they
expect me to be outrageous. Whether they would want
to actually observe such behaviour, I'm not quite sure,
but they certainly enjoy the telling. It somehow means
to them that I am not en route for the grave, that I have
vigorous life within me still, that they do not yet have
to worry about my survival. As I play the fool now, I
can still hear the 'Mum, Mum' phrase in my ears. But
it is no longer said with restraining embarrassment but
with delight and pride.

With that goodwill within me I no longer wake each
morning with dread or misery at sour relationships or
heavy, unappreciated workloads. It is good to have the
rat race behind me. As I face each day I can be a slob
about the housework if I choose, I don't have to fight
over radio or TV programmes, and can sing along
without embarrassment.

It all sounds complacent but it isn't. Don't think I

have no regrets. Of course I have missed opportunities, said the wrong thing, made the wrong choice. What is different for me at this time of my life is that I am not living a life of 'if – only's and regrets. What's past is past and the future is precious. I still have ambitions though I have a different goal from that of reaching the pinnacle of Everest. I may yet ski cross country, although I've left the slalom a bit late. I may yet do the meandering trip through France without a phrase book, even if it means learning the language first. I may yet make new friendships as I have done in recent years. I may yet have the courage to jump off the high diving board. I may yet make the most supremely delicious Baked Alaska. I may yet create a tapestry picture which I feel good enough to enter in a public exhibition. I may yet write a poem which I can truly feel is lyrical.

That is the true essence of what growing old disgracefully means to me – testing my personal frontiers, breaking down my self-built barriers.

GOODBYE TO ALL THAT
Shirley

No more periods, no more pain,
No more trying to be gloriously vain.

No more worrying day by day
When the kids are late and stay away.

No more striving after unreal wishes
No more sinks of dirty dishes.

No more menopause, no more flushes
No more adolescent crushes.

No more darning children's socks
No more chasing round the clock.

No more cleaning others' messes
No more backcombing unruly tresses.

No more arguing day by day
What to wear and what to say.

No more belief that men are stronger
Women are tough and we live longer.

No more victim, no more affairs
No more flaunting of physical wares.

No more pretence, this is me
No sleeping princess nor false modesty.

What I am is what I do
Even if it won't please you.

No more leaving things unsaid
No more wishing I was dead.

No more guilt, no more scorn
I may be old – but I'm glad I was born.

WHAT IT MEANS TO BE DISGRACEFUL
Anne

I am unlearning so many messages from childhood, and learning new ways of thinking and being. This old woman does not want to be nice, good, unselfish at all times, always putting others before herself and worrying about what other people think. I realise that there's no benefit, little pleasure or thanks to be received or earned from that behaviour. Now I want to put those things aside and try something new, something risky, and not worry whether my behaviour should meet with approval or not.

So, starting from this new premise, where does this old woman want to go, what do I want to do? Well, I want to try new experiences, aim to try something new every day. It need only be something small, tasting a new food, travelling to the end of the route with my bus-pass, wearing different colours together, singing out loud in the street, or something more momentous – living on a long boat, loving women, being more assertive. The small things are not too difficult to manage and add an exciting quality to a life to be lived in the present.

Now, I am having more fun than I remember having in years, and wondering how my children would respond to seeing their mother dancing and doing a 'knees-up' in the swimming pool, singing, giggling and playing silly games. I feel I have recaptured, or perhaps felt for the first time, an aliveness, a connection with childish enjoyment, of fun and absurdity, which might seem very shocking to my children. My daughter is envious when I go travelling in exotic places, when I spend my days of retirement doing what I want to do without any external pressures. Would she feel embarrassed to see this letting go of dignity and propriety?

I feel I have fitted in for too long with other people's expectations of what I should be, and, quite honestly, whether my children like it or not will not make one jot of difference. I intend to go on in the same way, doing something new, becoming a little more disgraceful each day. I want my children to be proud of me, but not at the expense of giving up any part of this wonderful present life!

KILL THE CAT *Barbara*

The damned cat!
A metaphor
For all the weights we tether to our ankles
To hold us to the ground.
I can't do that because ...
  – I'm just too old to try
  – I might look a fool
  – the family would not like it
  – my friends would not approve
  – I must think of the needs of others
  – the children might need me
AND – I can't leave the cat!

BUT – It's your turn now.
Free yourself and take to the air.
Spread your wings,
Allow yourself to fly ...
  – you are never too old to try
  – so what if you lose your dignity
  – the family will still love you
  – think of your own needs
  – the children will be freed
AND – if you can't make arrangements for the
  cat, it has had a long and happy life and it's your
  turn now.

BAMBOO TREKKING *Anne*

When two younger work colleagues asked me to join them on a six-week trip to Thailand, travelling with back-packs, I hesitated. I was 60 and just about to retire, I had never carried a back-pack, and my previous holidays had been organised throughout and were usually in comfortable hotels.

Knowing I might never get the chance again, I said 'yes' and subsequently enjoyed the most adventurous and exciting journey of my life.

The highlight of the trip was three days living and travelling downriver on a bamboo raft in the north of Thailand: four women (a young Japanese woman joined us) on this small, frail craft, looked after by two Thai raftsmen who steered the raft, one at each end, and cooked for us.

The country we travelled through was inhabited by isolated hill tribes, one of whom we visited, but for most of the way there was no sign of human habitation, just rice fields and forests. The raftsmen spoke no English. We were completely cut off from civilisation on a river that sometimes glided gently, sometimes fizzed and spurted (the 'rapids'). The silence was complete.

The first night, our cooks barbecued chicken over a roaring fire on the riverbank, cooked rice and noodles over a small stove. They cut up pineapple, papaya, bananas. The night was cold and very cramped, a heavy mist descended over the river, the floor was hard, cold came up through the cracks. The 'toilet' – a bamboo screen perched precariously on the side of the raft, contained two thick poles on which to stand and squat.

It was in the early hours of the first morning that I thought that I had made a terrible mistake in coming – my friends managed not to laugh when I said miserably 'I'm not spending another night on this raft.' But there was nowhere to go! As the sun rose on another perfect day, reflecting its rays in the quiet pools of the river, we set off again. That day we visited hot springs where the cleansing waters restored my equilibrium, we saw elephants being washed and scrubbed in the river, and I knew that I did not want to miss a moment of this unforgettable journey. I slept soundly the second night despite the discomfort, and continued to experience more magic sights and wonderful adventures.

AN 'AWAY' DAY *Edith*

'Don't you think you are being selfish?' queried a friend of mine when she learned about my impending trip to the Hen House for a Growing Old Disgracefully course. The remark arose when my husband, wishing to make arrangements for himself during my absence, asked her for information about possible courses for that period. 'Selfish' is not the word I would now use, 'disgraceful' perhaps, since in the context of my present life I'm making efforts to be more aware of my own needs and catering for them. In the process I am attempting not to make life too difficult for those who depend on me.

As I approach my 75th birthday, I find I need increasingly to stimulate and replenish my resources and energies. Where better than away from the everyday patterns and into other areas with old or new friends, having fun or engaged in challenging activities. On my return I have a good deal more to contribute to our combined lives besides feeling good about myself, my confidence improved.

At the behest of our children and grandchildren, I have made a good start in taping my personal history. They are all interested in the minutiae of my life especially the early days when the life styles and activities for young people were so different. A friend is assisting me, asking the pertinent questions, drawing me out and onwards. It stimulated her to reflect upon a comparable period in her life; there were tears as well as laughter as we shared our stories.

Freeing myself from the notion that the only approach to ageing was to accept it quietly, not making a fuss, has been a revelation. Learning that it is never too late, regardless of age, to make new friends has assisted greatly in achieving this freedom.

Last summer five women from our writing group went off on a day trip to Boulogne. We came together at Charing Cross station, took the train to Folkestone, then the boat across the Channel, arriving around midday. We had about six hours in France and were determined to exploit it to the full, which of course we did. No buses for us, we walked up the steep hill to the top of the town, purchasing some French bread to sustain us on the way. We had a gargantuan lunch in a restaurant garden, saw the town sights and wound our way down to the lower end of town with barely enough time left for supermarket shopping. Sitting on deck, during the return trip, slightly fatigued but pleased with ourselves, we felt as though we had been on a holiday

It was a hilarious day with laughter coming, going and during. Everything that could go wrong did; we were given the wrong tickets, we lost tickets, forgot passports, got on the wrong conveyance, but we blarneyed our way through each step of the way. It's not a trip I would have taken on my own and it would be too strenuous for my husband. If it had not been for the group not only would I have missed the occasion, but my husband would have missed out on his French apple tart!

Here is the song we wrote about the day. We might mention that in the week following, Sealink shut down its Folkestone office. We will forever believe that it was dealing with us that did them in.

A SONG TO THE TUNE OF
'Oh Dear, What Can the Matter Be'
Barbara and Maxine

Oh, dear, what a wonderful circumstance,
Five old women went off for a day in France,
In sandals and T-shirts and comfortable baggy pants
What a disgraceful affair!

The first one to get there she was Edith Redstone
She stood on the platform and waited there all alone,
Along came a gust and oh where had her ticket gone?
Gone with the wind and the air!

The second old woman, Anne, found herself in a spot,
Looked in her handbag – her passport she had forgot!
She travelled without one and somehow did not get
*   caught*
Nobody knew she was there!

The next one was Maxine who came from the USA,
She travelled to France in the hope of a quiet day.
Where was her ticket? She lost it – oy vay, oy vay!
She nearly paid double the fare!

The next thing that happened I'm sure that you'll
*   never guess,*
Got to the ship and then found we were ticketless,
The Paddington office had landed us in a mess!
Another disgraceful affair!

Five old Jewish women we searched for a perfect lunch
Not chicken soup but a rich shellfish dish to crunch,
A gargantuan meal was the choice of this hungry
*   bunch,*
Good thing our mothers weren't there!

The fourth ageing woman is our Shirley Meredeen,
Racing ahead she's our fast-moving leaderene!
The rest of us, panting, arrive after she's just been –
We can just see the back of her hair!

'What shall we buy?' as we raced to the nearest shop,
Wine, coffee and olives and Camembert cheese on top,
Then schlepping it back to the ship we all thought
  we'd drop,
Our feet started feeling the wear!

At the end of this long day our poor women nearly
  died,
Five minutes left and we're ordered to stand aside!
'Ridiculous nonsense, we're going ahead,' we cried
'We've not got a moment to spare.'

Down through the underpass Shirley was in the van,
After her, flailing and flapping our bags we ran.
'Wrong boat,' cried Maxine. 'Well, where can ours be?
  cried Anne.
'That must be it over there.'

Back in Folkestone we climbed on the bus with
  euphoria.
The staff of Sealink said 'Thank God there's no more
  o' ya.'
No-one told us the train went non-stop to Victoria
So once more we ran here to there!

Once on the train Barbara said, 'There must be a
  song,
Just let me write it, it won't take me very long
To relate how disgracefulness overcomes every wrong!'
They certainly knew we were there!

A FANTASY CORRESPONDENCE
Irene Smithe

From Bernard Barnes to his sister Elizabeth in Canada:

4th January

Dear Liz,

Many thanks for your letter and all the parcels – everyone was delighted. Jane and the kids are writing separately.

We had the usual sort of Christmas but, to tell you the truth, I am a bit worried about Mother since she came back from that Growing Old Disgracefully course. She's fine physically but she's behaving very oddly. Taken to wearing peculiar clothes for instance. We arranged to meet some friends in the White Hart for New Year drinks and thought it would be nice for Mother to come along with us (though of course this caused baby-sitting problems and we had to pay through the nose to get anybody). She turned up in pink pantaloons with a brilliant jacket all the colours of the rainbow. Jane says it was beautifully knitted but I must tell you, the whole effect was awfully embarrassing. Then there's the flat. I thought she really liked it when we built the granny-flat extension, but now she wants to throw out most of the furniture and pictures and get something different. She thinks she can redecorate it herself but I bet she'll be wanting me to help her. She's joined her art class again but now it's not those delicate water-colours that everybody liked so much. She's on to oils now, large abstracts in mysterious purples and grays, and – you'll never believe this – she's done a mural on her bathroom wall, full of the most peculiar nude figures intertwining like something in a Hindu temple. Really erotic, if not actually pornographic. I asked her how she could invite friends into the flat in the circumstances and she said 'Oh, they love it'.

Now she's having music lessons, learning to play - guess what - the saxophone. Good job the house is big enough for us not to hear the noise. The kids think it is great and want to learn too but I'm certainly not forking out for that. Gran can teach them if she likes. Nicky says Gran must on no account come with us to the school play if she is going to wear her weirdo clothes, so Jane has got to have a word with her about it. I wish you weren't so far away Liz. You have much more influence with Mother than I do, or Jane. Mother and Jane are always polite to each other but there's a certain hostility underneath I'm afraid.

No special news. Mother's Christmas present to us was some new roses for the garden. Must go and put them in while the weather is fine.

Love from us all, *Bernard*

Bernard to Elizabeth:

15th June

Dear Liz,

Thanks for your letter and the photograph. The cabin up in the Rockies looks wonderful - such trees, such views to wake up to every morning. I bet you are terribly fit. We are making do with a camp site in Brittany this year but not until the end of August. Too much work at the office for me to absent myself just yet.

Talking of holidays, what do you think Mother chose to do? She booked up for a sailing course down on the Solent somewhere. I ask you! An all-women affair. Apparently they never asked her age, only insisted on proper insurance cover, which was just as well as she slipped going down the companion way (in a hurry to get to the galley she said, as it was her turn to do the cooking) and broke her ankle. Arrived home with her leg in plaster and a couple of crutches. You can imagine Jane wasn't too pleased, she'd only just got over Tim's mumps. And Mother wasn't a bit contrite, just proud of not being seasick and planning to go back next summer. Over my dead body I said, which of course led to an argument. It seems she and Dad had a sailing dinghy once, before we were born and she's convinced she's a born sailor. Anyway, she's confined to her flat at the moment, practising the sax and working on her knitting – another one of those huge, shapeless, multi-coloured things that people turnround and stare at. We hear her stumping around on the crutches a good bit so she'll no doubt be negotiating the stairs any day now. She's reading Simone de Beauvoir! Honestly Liz, what do you think has got into her?

Actually, I was wondering if you might feel inclined to invite her over for a visit later in the year? Perhaps you could persuade her to act her age. I wouldn't mind paying the fare if she says she can't afford it. Of course it's up to you. I haven't said anything to her about it.

No special news. Jane and the boys send their love,

Bernard

Elizabeth to Bernard:

20th October

Well, Big Brother Bernard! I can see why you wanted to get rid of Mama for a bit. Not exactly the lady I remember from five years ago. When I climbed on to that plane at Heathrow I waved goodbye to a neat little person with nicely waved hair, a tailored suit and two rows of pearls. And who do I meet at our brand new neighbourhood airport? A wild woman who seems to have dropped off Cloud Nine, in baggy trousers, red boots, a red raincoat and assorted shawls and carrier bags. she was very tired and went straight to bed but had quite recovered by the next day and never stopped firing questions at me. I had to cough up the whole history of Canada in one easy lesson, not to mention potted biographies of my friends. One time we skirted round the edge of a real King Size row because I wouldn't talk about what happened to my marriage. I had to point out that being a mother did not include the right to pry. Do you have that trouble with her? But of course you wouldn't, you and Jane being the ideal couple, I suspect, in which case it wouldn't arise. Anyway I think she got the point. I've taken a week's leave to be with her and ferry her around to see the sights and into the city but next week I've got to go back to work. She says she'll cope and will enjoy being on her own. Unfortunately I haven't got to know many people locally, it's difficult in an apartment block, but I've introduced her to the local pensioners' group and most days some of them are down at the Community Centre, so I don't think she'll be lonely.

I'll report again soon. Love to all,

Liz

Elizabeth to Bernard:

10th November:

Dear Bernie,

Things have taken rather a disastrous turn. Mother made friends with the pensioners all right but with a bit too much enthusiasm. The next thing I knew, they had taken her with them on a hare-brained excursion to a conference of this US organisation called the Gray Panthers, being held in a hotel at Niagara Falls. I don't know much about them but by all accounts they are one hundred per cent militant (based on the Black Panthers I suppose) and campaign on every controversial issue under the sun, not just pensioners' rights – medicare, race discrimination, the third world, you name it, they're out there demonstrating. I didn't want her to go but short of locking her up, what could I do? And another thing, I think she's drawing too much money out of her bank account – it's so easy now that everything is plastic and international. Do you know how much she has actually got left of Father's money? If she blows it all you'll be left holding the baby – or rather the granny. I haven't got two cents to rub together.

Next day: Just had a phone call from Mother from Washington DC! Apparently some of them flew down there on Saturday to take part in a march against homelessness. It all got out of hand, they were attacked by hoodlums from the American National Party and then by the cops. Mama spent the night at police headquarters locked up with God knows who. They let them out next morning but she sounds very shaken. Anyway she's due back here tonight. I can't believe this is happening. You may well ask what our old folk are coming to. It used to be Youth with a capital Y that caused all the trouble (remember when we were Youth?) Now I suppose they are all stoned up to the eyeballs and don't give a damn.

Must go now. Will keep you posted. Love,

Liz

Mrs Mary Barnes to Bernard, 15th November:

My dear Bernie,

As Liz told you over the phone, I shall be arriving Thursday of next week. I'm sorry to have caused her all this worry. I shall lead a quiet life from now on but I wouldn't have missed my transatlantic experience for anything, and I'm so grateful to you and Liz for making it possible. One thing I must tell you. Liz does not know about this, but a Canadian friend of mine is coming to Heathrow on the same flight and I have invited him to stay a while with me. I know there isn't much room but the studio couch is quite comfortable. Hope you don't mind. It won't inconvenience you and Jane. He's a quiet person, though rather striking to look at – very tall, though he's got a bit of a stoop (he's sixty something), dark complexion, very dark eyes, long hair. He's a Native American (Red Indian to you), teaches history and is something of a specialist in the story and culture of his own nation (don't use the word tribe to him, will you, it has such imperialist overtones). It's terrible what happened to them but he's awfully wise somehow. I'm sure you will like him. We met at the Gray Panthers conference and then in Washington we got arrested together. It was pretty nasty but it certainly helps you to get to know people. I'm really looking forward to being home again. The boys will love meeting Jack. His real name is Son of White Eagle. There's some research he wants to do in London about early settlers in Canada.

Must go now, see you next week.

Much love, Mama

BIRTHDAY PARTY *Shirley*

At my sixtieth birthday there were over 100 guests, each of whom had played an important part in my life. There were schoolfriends from 45 years ago, family, work colleagues from the past 20 years and sister students from Open University and WEA classes. There were gurus I had met along life's path, friends from fun times and support groups. Some people from each of the groups had not known each other before. Some found links across ages and diversities.

These different sections formed a giant cobweb of friendship, support and learning which has sustained and nourished me. Different parts of the network came to the fore to different degrees and at different times. I give to and take from them all according to our mutual needs and one part does not take precedence over another; they overlap and act as counterbalances.

My friendships and networks have not just happened. Throughout my life I have valued people and tried to keep in touch even when life has caused separations. My efforts have turned out to be a good investment. I feel blessed to have a network of family, old friends, ex-colleagues, cornershop acquaintances and new friends that I continue to garner, but this hasn't happened by my sitting back and expecting the phone to ring or living through my children's lives.

I enjoy solitude at times, but I also enjoy making withdrawals from my bank of friends, especially when I have something to share. Sharing does not diminish but strengthens me. My wish for other women is that they will give each other the nourishment, energy and courage to grow into old age feeling as lucky as I do.

NETWORKS *Barbara*

Any woman who sews
or knits, or weaves,
blends colours in a tapestry
or creates a patchwork quilt,
knows by the feel
that a single thread is weak
but the weaving,
the blending,
the intertwining
with many others
makes it strong.

Any woman alone,
without friends
to sustain her,
to nurture and support,
to hold with loving arms,
like a single thread, is weak.
But the weaving,
the loving,
the nurturing of others,
the networks of friendship
make her strong.

HERE'S TO VIRGINIA *Maxine*

'This is what I miss, Cordelia; not something that's gone, but something that will never happen. Two old women giggling over their tea.' Margaret Atwood, *Cat's Eye*

Virginia and I always had plans for the future that included each other. We were going to be disgraceful old women together, living spontaneously and with abandon.

On the surface, she and I seemed to have little in common, yet we were best friends for more than 20 years. When I try to think of what it was that held us together, I can only believe that it was our shared sense of what we called 'madness'. We both relished the absurd; we loved to do the unexpected. Despite, or perhaps because of our previous years of being respectable suburban wives and mothers, we still liked to play, and we wanted to experience (almost) everything. Of course we had our barriers – children, money, responsibilities – but somehow we managed to work a whole lot of fun into our single-parent way of life.

As I look back on our years of closeness, I remember times when we saved each other from depression, loneliness, difficult family situations. In the ways we were alike we provided familiarity and comfort for each other; in the ways we were different and saw the world through the filters of our disparate experiences, we provided a balance for one another.

Even after we drifted off to different parts of the world, we felt the other's support. We would get together for an occasional visit or go off on holiday together, and it would seem we had never been apart. We often went months without communicating. We didn't have to – we took our friendship and our future together for granted.

Last summer Virginia died of lung cancer at the age of 63. She always said that her heavy smoking habit would be her downfall, but since none of her attempts to quit lasted long, she finally made a conscious decision to go on enjoying her cigarettes and daily wine even if it meant a shorter life. Selfishly, I wanted her to change her lifestyle so that we could enjoy our old age together. I'm sad to lose that dream, but I respect that it was her life about which to make her own choices.

I didn't know about her illness until after she died. I was staying in England for the summer and had planned to call her as soon as I got re-settled back home. The last time I spoke with her, we made tentative plans to meet, possibly in Italy, for a disgraceful holiday together before I ended my sabbatical leave year. We had so many things still to talk about that were waiting until we saw each other again, but that never happened.

What I regret most is not being with her at the end; not that I could have forestalled her death, but just to be able to send her off with a cheer. I hear from her son that in her last moments she dreamed of a band of

French Foreign Legionnaires having a party, toasting each other (with wine, of course) then putting down their glasses and walking towards a bright white light. I hope her final fantasy means that wherever she is now, she and the Frenchmen are having fun. I'll wager she's saving a spot for me.

Virginia Lowery attended our July 1989 'Growing Old Disgracefully' course. This piece is dedicated to her memory.

FRIENDSHIP *Barbara*

Mist shrouds the island,
Foghorns mourn.
Through tapping keys
Thoughts find their way.
In the distance
Somebody hums
A gentle tune.
A page is turned.
Companionable peace
Wraps each of us
In warmth
And life is good.

There are no oughts
No musts or shoulds.
Through sharing thoughts
And fears and pain
Each of us finds
The simple path,
The way to hear
The gentle humming,
The way to make
The small changes.
As we grow old
Life will be good.

CHAPTER FIVE

Sex and Sensuality

'Would you cut up the stewing steak for me?'
'Certainly, since you are so young and pretty.'
'But if I weren't young and pretty?'
'Then you'd have to go elsewhere!'

This bantering exchange that took place recently between Shirley and her butcher speaks volumes about how youth and beauty and male admiration are women's bargaining cards. The butcher expected Shirley to take it as the ultimate compliment to be told, however jokingly, that she looked young and sexually desirable in a man's eyes. This is a graphic illustration of the subtle ways in which women are given the message that our power declines with age.

Looking young and conventionally attractive is especially crucial to heterosexual women who feel insecure about holding on to a man or finding a new one. Jokes abound about husbands who want to trade their wives in for newer models or exchange a 60-year-old wife for two in their thirties. The truth that this so-called humour obscures only serves to reinforce an ageing woman's feelings of vulnerability. Each wrinkle, each grey hair, each added pound becomes cause for alarm. Think of the industries that flourish by preying on women's insecurities by exhorting us to buy this cream or that potion, this diet or that exercise plan, with the promise that it will make us look younger.

There is no product that can change how old you actually are – no matter how you feel or how you look.

Have you ever caught a glimpse of yourself in a mirror and, for an instant, thought 'That can't be me, I'm not that old!'? When you meet school friends do you feel that they have aged much more than you have? When you ask for a pensioner's discount are you disconcerted when your right to claim it is not questioned? Somewhere along the line your inner and outer selves have lost congruence, the inner you feels just as it did before but the outer you has aged without your noticing it.

Love Your Body, Love Yourself

It is sad that so many old women have learned to hate their bodies, to be ashamed of them. It is not by coincidence that references to mirrors keep appearing in our writings. Mirrors show us the reality of our wrinkles and sags, a reality which we've been taught to despise.

To grow old disgracefully means not believing that you are a failure or that somehow it is your own fault because your body is changing with age. You can learn to like yourself and your body according to your own standards and you can refuse to submit to the tortures of trying to mould your body into something it is not. You can accept both the inner and the outer you, even when they seem incongruent. You can laugh with other women as you find common experiences of ageing bodies.

If you have had operations or amputations, or if you live with a chronic illness or condition, it may be difficult to like your body as it is and we certainly are not suggesting denial. We are saying that at least some part of our discomfort with our bodies comes from being taught to see them as deficient, as not good enough. The image that we are told to strive for never includes ageing, infirmities or evidence of vulnerability to emotional or physical ailments. As an alternative to measuring yourself against this supposedly ideal image, you can acknowledge and mourn what is lost while you thank the scars and disabilities for reminding you that you are a survivor, ageing as disgracefully as possible under your particular circumstances.

For any woman the first step toward accepting and loving your own body must be to learn to feel comfortable with it. Allow yourself to enjoy being naked walking around your own room or house or flat if that's appropriate. Don't flinch from mirrors. Smile at yourself if that feels right for you.

An exercise that is helpful in providing a positive body image is to stand or sit (nude, if you can) in front of a full-length mirror. Really look at yourself, every part of you, slowly. Think about each part of your body and all the wonderful ways in which it has served you well. You may feel silly and uncomfortable at first but the more you do this the better you will feel about your body, whatever your size, shape or appearance.

This is the only body you've got. It *is* you, just as vitally as your inner core is you. If you hate it, it is yourself you are hating and you will not be able to move forward into your disgraceful old age. And if, like most women, you have been conditioned to believe that sex appeal depends on conventional physical attractiveness, then it is easy to see how your body image affects your sexuality.

Bodies and Sex

As our group talked and wrote about our ageing bodies we realised that it was impossible to separate how we feel about our bodies from how we express our sexuality, or whether we express it at all. It was not always easy to discuss sex and even more difficult to commit our words to paper for others to read. As you might expect, this chapter evolved only after we had built up confidence in ourselves and trust in each other. The more we shared, however, the more we understood that 'older women and sexuality' is not a contradiction in terms.

Speaking openly in a group about sex and bodies may be difficult for women of our generation because most of us were socialised to be 'nice girls'. You may recognise some of the lessons:

> Nice girls do not talk about sex; nice girls do not have sexual appetites; nice girls grow up to be nice ladies who service their husband's sexual needs (which of course will be stronger than their own); nice ladies never cast aspersions on their husband's sexual prowess, to him or to anyone else; there is no sex outside marriage – before, during or after; and, of course, women can be loving friends but never sexual partners.

As difficult as it may be, talking honestly about our bodies and about sex breaks down unnecessary taboos and clears some of the obstacles to growing old disgracefully. It is another way to use our own voices to create our own definitions for what it means to be sexual as we age. The more you listen to other women's voices, the more you begin to recognise and appreciate the options that are open to you as you live longer than your partner, as you grow old with a partner, or as you remain unpartnered by choice or circumstance.

We found much variation within our group in the ways we felt about and expressed our sexuality. One woman has chosen lesbianism; another suggested that masturbation is a preferable alternative or at least a supplement to love-making with another person, others thought masturbation not at all comparable to the pleasures of intercourse; one of us is opting for celibacy, others are having to accept celibacy but have not ruled out the possibility of sex, another would like more sex with her ageing husband; some of us are re-assessing our needs and wondering about bisexuality. We agree that experiencing sensual pleasures is important in its own right, whether within the context of sex or not.

We have tried to be honest in our writing. If you can identify with what we say, or if we can make it easier for you to think, write or talk about your own body and how you want to express your sexuality, then we will have succeeded in taking one more step together towards growing old disgracefully.

A SENSE OF SELF *Barbara*

Have you ever noticed the competent confidence of little girls at about nine or ten? They seem to have such a sense of themselves, they are so self-possessed. But so many of us lose that confidence when we reach adolescence. What happens to females to separate them from that confident core? I remember so clearly that wonderful feeling of agility as I clambered over rocks on the beach or played ball up against a wall. I remember how my Clark's sandals gripped the ground as I ran and jumped.

Yet by the time I was about 15 I had learned that my body was somehow not quite good enough, that it did not measure up to society's image of female beauty. I learned not to like my own body; it was flat where it should have curved and wide in the hips when it was fashionable to be slim. I knew very little about sex and I did not feel myself to be 'sexually attractive'. My mother had prided herself on being progressive and always answering my questions – but I had not known the questions to ask! It is hard to believe how ignorant I was about sex when I first met the man I later married. I was 19 and he was 29. Shortly before we began sleeping together, after a passionate embrace, he said that he had nearly ejaculated. 'Ejaculated?' I thought. 'Why is he telling me that?' I thought he meant that he had nearly exclaimed 'Good God!' or 'For heaven's sake!'

I enjoyed sex within our marriage but later realised how inhibited I had been, largely through ignorance. It was only as my marriage ended and I began a relationship with another man that sex became something overwhelmingly wonderful. I was in my late thirties, my husband had fallen in love with one of my friends and my self-image was at an all-time low. I felt myself to be unattractive and unlovable. The joy of a lover was like a magic potion, I blossomed and shone. I began to love my own body as much as I loved his lean body; we fitted together. The ending of this relationship was as devastating as the end of my marriage. The double rejection left me lower in my own estimation than ever before.

The unexpected life-line came in the shape of an old loved married friend whose wife felt my sadness so poignantly that she had the strength and confidence to share him. It is remarkable that we have sustained our loving friendship over the last 20 years and he and I were lovers for ten years. It was sex without passion but with a great deal of fun and lovingness. It was so good to be loved and touched, to be seen as a sexual being when I was struggling to keep the family together, run the home and hold down a job. He added the spice that made life worthwhile.

I have had many sexual encounters since then; the last with a much younger man made me very aware of my ageing body. It is one thing to age alongside a partner, the stretch-marks and thickening hips are mementoes of your shared lives. But presenting your body to somebody new is an alarming prospect. Women have so few role-models of older bodies, the cult of youth is so pervasive. We have been conditioned to look at our own bodies through the lens of the advertiser's camera. But I have come to see my old woman's body as beautiful in its own way. The full breasts which fed my children, the well-rounded hips, the silver stretch-marks on my round belly showing where my babies grew curled in my soft womb, the legs that carried me through pregnancies and endless treks to and from schools and shops and up and down stairs, the arms that have worked and nurtured and comforted. Now I fit my own body, I no longer long for it to be different. We should learn not to compare our bodies or devalue them or look at them through other people's eyes. We should be proud of our bodies, they are wonderful.

THE BODY BEAUTIFUL *Anne*

It was not until I was about 52, part of a group of women meeting to explore our sexuality, that I became wholly aware of my body. This may sound strange coming from a woman who was married for 25 years and with two grown-up children, and it does not mean that I did not enjoy sex with my ex-husband, because I did. It means that I was not sure of my anatomy, or how it functioned; I could not be sure whether I had orgasms or not, or of the stages of orgasm.

With the guidance of an experienced leader we learned various exercises to strengthen our pelvic muscles. We did 'homework' every night, then shared our experiences and feelings in the next group meeting. We were asked to find a small part of our home (and this was not easy for women with partners or children) and to make it our own special place, with rugs, cushions, candles, flowers, anything to make it special. Then, after a bath, to spend an allotted time, at the same time of every day, in that place. We were invited to look at our bodies in a mirror; to touch, lick our bodies, smell our bodies; become intimate with that part of ourselves which had been with us from the day we were born but which we had been taught to ignore.

We were invited to dress in flimsy clothing, to fantasise, to make ourselves feel sexy, to masturbate to orgasm. I remember the first time I masturbated as part of my evening pleasure period (I had never had 'permission' to do so before). I gradually got more and more excited till I reached orgasm and felt the warm surge of blood through my body. I burst into tears of gratification and delight. I shared that experience by telling the group at our next meeting.

Soon after this I joined an intuitive massage group of men and women, where, after initial hesitation and embarrassment, we massaged one another in the nude. The giving, and the feel of another human body under my hands, was a wonderful experience, a mutual exchange of energy.

My need for bodily contact after the break-up of my marriage when I was 50, directed me to the sexuality and massage groups and then into a relationship with a woman – a body created in the same image as my own, a woman with beautiful breasts, soft curves, a rounded lovely body and long golden hair.

Now that I am on my own I love and appreciate my body. I exercise it, keep my muscles toned; I try not to overfill it; I try to be kind to it. I have occasional periods of yearning for an 'other' but I have had no intimate relationship for over four years, except with myself, and that feels good.

When a great adventure is offered, you don't refuse it.
Amelia Earhart

NO MORE WOLF WHISTLES   *Shirley*

When I was a girl
The wolf whistle call
Gave me a shiver of delight.
I walked tall.
My eyes shone with the recognition of womanhood
Fast approaching,
In which the admiration of men promised much
  excitement.

When I grew woman tall
The wolf whistle call
Became an insult.
I was seen as an object for observation alone.
Men's perception of beauty rang hollow
As my internal self sought approbation
More needfully than the mirror's reflection.

As I grow old
The wolf whistle call
Is a thing of the past.
Both regret and delight.
The looks alone that attracted are gone.
Other compensations satisfy instead.

Age brings regrets,
But for this relief much thanks.
I can do without the falseness of superficial
  appreciation,
Skin deep alone.
The affection I now receive is for me,
The real me.
This was worth waiting for.

THE MIRROR *Shirley*

My bathroom has a wall-to-wall mirror. I bought the flat when I was 55 and the mirror almost deterred me from the purchase. Could I bear to see my ageing wrinkled body at full frontality every time I had a bath? Should I compromise by bathing in the dark or should I face the reality of the bumps, sagging lines and over-ripe flesh that was the physical part of me? It would be hard to acknowledge this ageing body daily as it deteriorated in the years ahead, but I was resigned to accepting that this was my lot. Not a pretty sight. Poor but mine own.

Imagine the shock to my system just a few years later, faced by the gazing eyes of a man 21 years my junior, as I bathed. Earlier in the evening he had asked if he could sleep with me. His desire had startled but delighted me and when I said yes I had not thought through the implications of his examination of my body. When the bathroom door opened I was doubly exposed – both to the mirror which threatened me with cruel honesty and to him. I gasped with embarrassment, instinctively drew my arms in against my breasts and shivered nervously. But he knelt down at my side and gently prised my arms open, looked at me with delight, smiled and began to stroke me gently. No part of my body escaped his hands. Slowly I began to relax, to pulsate with excitement and to begin to experience my most sensual time for many years.

So began a year of bodily pleasure, divorced from emotional attachment. I did not hang on his every word nor experience a missed heartbeat when the telephone rang. Each loving meeting was complete as an individual set of moments. I was grateful to him for this reawakening after ten years of celibacy after my divorce, but I had no investment in its continuity. Every time we met I reminded him that his hands should be on a body younger and more beautiful than mine.

Seven years earlier I had helped to mount a campaign to resist his deportation as an illegal immigrant and since then he had completed a university career and gone on to gainful employment. The time we spent together felt to me like his expression of gratitude for saving him from a return to persecution and the threat of death. He seemed to see me as his saviour and his gratitude got in the way of this encounter becoming anything deeper. Not only did the experience seem incestuous (indeed my adult sons had visited him in prison those years before), but also I found it hard to accept his loving me as anything more than his way of saying thank you.

As an older woman who had given all to a marriage through good times and bad, and to a career of helping others, I needed a relationship which gave me something more than bodily satisfaction, however gently caressing and arousing. The encounter felt too maternal and we shared too few interests to make it a fully satisfying relationship for me who, like many women of my age, had always found it hard to be sexual unless it was part of a total relationship.

However, for that one year I enjoyed his exploration of my body – it was obviously not as repulsive as I had thought. I no longer dreaded its exposure to his young eyes. He satisfied me sexually and it was a physical delight to feel his taut young body under my tracing hands. I had not anticipated such a thrill happening to me ever again. He had awakened in me those sexual urges which I had denied for so long. He taught me to separate physical satisfaction from the wholeness of body-mind satisfaction which had previously been my requirement. (It remains my ideal but I can accept the fact that such bliss may not be my lot again.)

The experience reminded me that I was still a person

with sexual needs despite the fact that I was now sixty, and that these needs would continue as I aged. At least I now feel less closed in than before and it feels OK to acknowledge my sexuality without the pangs of first love and teenage anguish. This was no 'toy-boy' experience but an episode of learning, rejuvenation and confirmation of me as a woman with sexual desires, no matter how I choose to satisfy them.

THE DREAM *Edith*

Kissing and being passionately kissed in return, locked in my husband's embrace, my body lovingly stroked to the pitch of arousal, I am ready, willing, able and waiting to be entered. What bliss! ... but what is happening, where am I? What is that ungodly sound? The penetrating noise is my husband snoring and I am having my recurring dream. I get up, go to the bathroom, have a walk around the flat, open the door to the garden, take a breath of hot, warm, cold or icy air depending on the season, and eventually go back to bed. To sleep, perhaps to dream again, or just to lie there pondering on how my sexual life has changed.

It is strange how the tide has turned during our long marriage. My sexual needs and satisfaction developed over the years while his diminished and now only occasionally flare up. There's lots of cuddles and hand-holding but not much of the ultimate satisfaction. It was not always thus, our seven-year age difference mattered not at all during a good part of our marriage. In the early days especially it enhanced our sexual relationship. He was more experienced and as I learned from him our marriage developed and improved.

There was one period of almost a year of abstinence for both of us when he became ill with a recurrence of tuberculosis, underwent a series of painful operations and then a long convalescence. My days were very full with two small children and daily visits to hospital but the nights were miserable, lying in bed alone with no warm body to caress, no excitement, just an emptiness. Regular sex had been very much a part of our marriage and the absence of it, and the loneliness left me feeling bereft.

He returned home on schedule just a year after the onset of his illness and we took up where we had left off. Bedtime was once more the pleasure it had been. But things do change and increasing age can affect the sexes differently, as it has us after 50 years of marriage, so we hold on to our memories and to the deep affection we have for one another.

UNTITLED *Barbara*

My lips are brushing my own shoulder,
How sweet the touch of skin on skin.
My fingertips explore the contours of my face.
There are no arms to hold me,
No soft caresses spring my skin to life.
So long, so long since I was touched with love.

THE SAUNA Shirley

Nakedness in the sauna steam
Brings confrontation with my dream.
Once lithe and supple body of mine
Is face to face with others so fine,
So young, so firm, such nubile breasts,
Such taut young tums and rounded bums.
We eye each other through misty haze
Compare our bodies, consider the days.
Which one is best? Do I pass their test?

As we chat and sweat
I gradually get
Closer to what I often forget.

I remember with some considerable pride
The labour my body fails to hide.
No wonder that my hips are wide.

The nestling children
The bustling day
The march for peace
The roll in the hay
The well-scrubbed floors
The knocking and pushing at long-closed doors
For jobs I needed to pay the rent
With tears and sweat and long lament.
This body could tell a tale or two
Without regret or need to be you.

I don't want to change my shape
Or hide my skin beneath a cape.
This well-worn body is really mine,
And for me that's perfectly fine.

PRIVATE PARTS *Mary*

At the age of 68 I am glad to be free of the worry and anxiety that sex and sexual encounters have meant for me. I smile at myself in the mirror, I like what I see, my face looks less lean and haggard when I smile ... vanity, vanity! I am determined not to put on a lot of weight. I dye my hair and I have been getting it permed recently. I enjoy clothes (I always notice what other women – but never men – are wearing). All this helps me in the sense of being in charge of my own self image. I know that I don't look young but I look good!

Until now I have never felt really happy with my own body. It fell so far short of what seemed the ideal. I carried round this idea of myself as a body with spindly legs, wide hips, well-padded. When someone said I had a good figure (I was 19 at the time) I was astonished as well as pleased. This was about the time I first found out about sex, how it worked, what a man's penis actually looked and felt like and the exquisite excitement when his hand found my genitals.

After four pregnancies, and, if I am honest, probably well before that, I found it difficult to feel the same excitement. I remember lying in bed beside my husband, having had sex (I can't say 'making love' because I did not feel that we had made love). He would fall asleep and I would lie awake wondering if he knew how miserable I felt. But he did not realise and never would or could.

My desire for sexual excitement had not gone away so I had affairs. Sometimes the sex was better than ever before but I never felt truly loved by any man, needed perhaps – but that is different. What are my alternatives now that I am no longer interested in a relationship with a man? I have always found that masturbation, one of the hardest words for women brought up like me to say, let alone write down, can be very satisfying. If sex is OK with a partner, why not on your own? Perhaps we need to give ourselves this kind of pleasure as we get older and other options fade. I also wonder if we are all potentially bi-sexual. I feel sure that, under different circumstances, my own sexuality could have developed differently. I grew out of the crush-on-other-girls stage, as so many of us did in our teens.

As I grow older it is sensuality not sexuality that matters. One of the greatest joys for me now is to hear music to dance to, to dance, dance on my own or with other women, circle dancing, folk dancing, making up your own dancing. The surprise, the magic is still there. Touching and seeing and smelling and tasting and hearing, the feel of the sun on my skin, the smell of honeysuckle in June, the taste of olives or cream cakes, the first sight of the sea!

On holiday this year came unexpectedly the chance to swim in a steamy indoor pool. I had never seen a place like it. No-one else was there, it was late in the evening. We had no swimming costumes with us, so we took off our clothes where we stood and plunged in. Warm, warm, gently we moved in the water and sang in the great hollow steamy chamber, three old women naked together. I am 68 I told myself, and swimming naked for the first time in my life! I looked up, some people from our party had gathered on the balcony, high above the water. They were watching us and it didn't matter two hoots!

People seem to think that you don't know anything about sex after you're 40 or 50. That's ridiculous. You know a great deal more about sex when you're 80 than when you're 40.　　　　　　　　　　　Mary Wesley

A HEALTHY WOMAN *Anne*

At 61 I feel myself to be a very lucky and healthy person. Or am I? Let's be honest.

Well, yes I am healthy, apart from my slight deafness, diminished eyesight, wheezy chest, thinning hair, thickening body, and all those twinges which seem to develop from nowhere on getting up in the morning, walking more than half a mile or even just sitting.

Have you ever had the embarrassment of mishearing and then asking all the wrong questions? Recently a work colleague said, or I thought she said, 'I am going to America in August.' My reply of 'How wonderful, business or pleasure?' brought a very strange look in response. When she told me that her statement had been 'I am getting married in August' I realised that it is better to ask for things to be repeated than to pretend to understand and risk replying inappropriately. But, of course, I am not deaf!

My eyesight gives me no problems at all. I do carry three pairs of glasses and I am continually changing from one pair to another, depending on whether I am reading a book, gazing at the distant horizon or just obscuring the bright, blinding rays of the sun. And when people look at me in my reading glasses and tell me that one lens is all misted, I have to explain that one lens is actually opaque and only by reading with one eye can I prevent seeing the print double since the second line hovers a few centimetres below the first, making the whole page indecipherable. Obviously no diminishment there!

I love walking, especially in hilly countryside. I love to put on heavy walking shoes and socks, put my knapsack on my back – with my three pairs of glasses, of course, plus binoculars for small distant objects, my inhaler, homeopathic remedies, several layers of extra clothing (my thermostat isn't what it was) and rainwear as I don't like getting wet, then I stride up grassy banks, rocky protuberances and winding paths. After about ten minutes I can hear a strange noise (even with my diminished hearing) and look around to see where it is coming from. Not from my companions, no stray sheep around, no insects croaking or whining. Oh no, it's me, or more correctly, my wheezing chest. Breathing becomes more difficult, I start to feel weak, I must sit down. I cough and splutter, use my inhaler. Just a temporary over-exertion!

I like to wash my hair every two or three days. Luckily it is very short and dries very quickly and takes about four minutes from the first shampoo to the final rinse. What takes another 15 minutes is collecting all the loose hairs which have lined the bath, fallen from the towel or clung to my shoulders, and gathering them into a ball to put in the waste-bin. What little is left on my head gets thinner every year and barely covers the bumps, however carefully I arrange the remaining tresses. My crowning glory has lost a little of its lustre!

Despite all these little problems, I am glad to say that I never put on weight. True, the scales register a few more pounds every year but you have to make allowances for any mechanical object to show increasing inaccuracy. And if my clothes feel a little tighter it means, of course, that in my attempt to remain clean and fresh-looking, they shrink a little every time they go through the wash or to the cleaners. A fine figure of a woman, so earthy, so rounded, so cuddly!

It is strange that, after a night of rest and relaxation, my first attempt to sit upright and then to stand or even walk, can feel so difficult. When I pull myself into a sitting position, there are creaking noises around the lower body. Surely I didn't go to bed with that stiff neck? As my feet reach the floor and try to support the weight of my body I am forced to sit down heavily on the edge of the bed – I am not sure my legs can cope with the task. Gradually the twinges subside, as though the cogs have been oiled and set in motion, and my body can face up to another day's challenges.

Please don't take this string of weaknesses as any diminishment due to ageing. I don't – and I should know!

REFLECTIONS *Barbara*

I have a trick I play each day
It leaves me comforted –
I never wear my glasses
When I first get out of bed.

And in my bathroom mirror
I peer with pleased surprise
At the gently blurred soft image
Through my short-sighted eyes.

Then later, washed and ready,
My glasses now in place,
I glance into the mirror
And see my mother's face.

MY BODY *Maxine*

My body is what she is; she is my body. I am she. The battle is over and I have emerged 'bloody but unbowed'. What a relief. If someone doesn't like my folds, my flabs, my breasts that sit on my fat belly, my veined and scarred and mottled skin, too bad. I am impressed that my body could rack up so many miles and still keep running.

Well, perhaps 'running' is a bit of a stretch. Walking, or sometimes crawling, might be more accurate. Who wants to run anyway? It only puts stress on out-of-commission joints, of which I have more each day. And why go fast, when time is doing that for me already?

My body still sees, though not as sharply as it might; still hears, but often with hilarious misunderstandings; still smells smells and tastes tastes well enough (and can still smell and taste good itself, if you want the sensual truth of it).

Take my breasts, for example. It has been a long while since I could call my breasts 'perky'. They don't stand up by themselves any more, these stretch-marked pendula that have given nourishment and pleasure to babies grown to men and women.

I remember becoming aware of my breasts for the first time at about age nine. I was 'beginning to develop' (one of those euphemisms I was taught to use for unspeakable bodily functions). There I was, guilelessly changing clothes in front of an assortment of relatives, when one uncle began pointing at me. I couldn't understand at first what caused them all to laugh and speak as if it had something to do with me. Then suddenly I knew, and without will I felt my shame rising to pull my hands over my tiny harbingers of womanhood.

I started menstruating that same year (oh, the euphemisms we learned for that one!) and my breasts kept right on growing. And growing. And growing. I learned ways to hide them: bras that flattened, school books carried in front of them. I was two years younger than my class-mates, having skipped grades, but even with their chronological advantage, I had the largest breasts.

As I was also the tallest, the least physically coordinated and the most self-conscious, I did not have a very loving relationship with my body and no-one did anything to dispel my anguish. Because we were poor I was often dressed in older cousins' made-over hand-me-downs, which were all too often inappropriate for my size and shape. The cousins were brunette, thin, short and flat-chested; I was blonde, tall, heavy and full-bosomed. They were all giggly, boy-attracting and ruffly. I was cerebral, unpopular and style-illiterate.

My sex education consisted of one admonition: Don't Do It. It was up to me to find out what 'IT' meant. On the other hand, I was supposed to do everything possible to exude sex appeal. To attract males (I knew of no other options) I was told: don't be too clever (boys don't like girls who are smart); listen but don't speak (boys want to talk about themselves so act impressed and encouraging); do whatever it takes to make your body into a male's version of ideal (spare no torture, wear high-heeled shoes, girdles, tight clothing).

Ah, the clothing! Young women today may think that Madonna invented pointed armour for breasts. Well, in the 1940s I was wearing bras that transformed my breasts into lethal weapons. They preceded me into a room by at least six bars of the latest Glenn Miller recording. And the girdles with suspenders were enough to discourage even the most ardent Romeo. I teetered on high heels, not realising at the time how I was ruining my back and feet, but I looked sexy, and that was all that mattered.

In the 1950s my breasts were busy with husband and

babies. They were more or less utilitarian. It wasn't until the hippies and feminists began to draw attention to how our bodies had been restricted that I was once again aware of my breasts.

Out went all the bras and girdles. What a relief! No more harnesses to encumber me. I could move freely. The liberation of my breasts from their armour became a metaphor for liberty and a society freed from oppression. So you see, in a way my breasts speak of a social history as well as a personal one. My breasts are political, as are all women's breasts, and not just because of style. If you do not believe me, start thinking about how much money our governments spend on research and how little of it is spent on finding the causes and cure for breast cancer. And why is it that our breasts can be used publicly to sell products and newspapers but when we nourish babies we must still do it in private or cover up discreetly?

What now for me? I wear bras again (but not girdles or high heels), not for style but for comfort. As I said, what used to perk now pends, so without a bra to separate flesh from flesh, I get a rash. Having become liberated in so many other ways, however my wearing a bra or not seems inconsequential.

I plan to use my precious remaining time and energy in other ways than trying to change or disguise my body. So when you see the large-sized, healthy, comfortable me on the streets, my body, breasts and all, will be taking up as much space as needed with no apology.

CHAPTER SIX

Disgraceful
To the End

Thus far we have written about the past and the present, and now it is time to look to the future. If growing old disgracefully implies living life to the full with joy and hope, we need to ask how that can be accomplished in our final years. It is one thing to talk about growing old disgracefully while you are still reasonably healthy and self-sufficient, but quite another to equate it with strokes, incontinence, failing eyesight, loss of hearing and all the other aches and pains which can accompany old age.

We certainly do not have any easy or glib answers to offer. Ageing has its drawbacks, its possible tragedies, and we would be irresponsible to suggest otherwise. And despite what we might like to believe, ageing is not 'all in the mind' but is a combination of bodily changes and attitudes towards those changes. Our bodies will continue through a natural ageing process whether or not we think it is fair, so what is a disgraceful old woman to do?

We have built the following suggestions by using all the letters of DISGRACEFUL TO THE END. Everything on the list assumes at least minimal physical mobility and little diminishment of mental faculties. We realise that there are diseases, such as Alzheimer's, and certain physical conditions that would preclude what we have to say, and we hope these will not be your lot, but the following suggestions include some things you can do now to make decisions while you are still able, just in case.

We hope you will have fun with our list, and that you will want to revise it, add to it, subtract from it, and make it your own according to your particular needs and circumstances.

D is for **DISCOVERY**, for no matter what your age or physical abilities, there is always more to discover about our miraculous universe and the people in it. **DISCUSS** what you **DISCOVER** with other people and you will remain interesting to be with. **DISPROVE** the old Freudian notion that old people cannot learn.

There are many classes and activities offered through a variety of organisations, some specifically for old people. There are books in large print or on tape if you need them. Try forming your own book or other type of discussion group with friends and neighbours. And for those of you who are addicted to crossword puzzles, now is your chance to justify your obsession, because there is some evidence that they keep the mind sharp. You can sometimes find them in large print too.

If you are mobile, take advantage of pensioners' concessions and enjoy the cultural activities in your area. There are often organised daytime trips offered through local centres. The important thing is to **DISCOVER** for yourself how to keep up with old interests or develop new ones, which brings us to . . .

I is for **INTERESTS**, **INTERACTIONS** and refusing to be **INVISIBLE**. When you **INTERACT** with others around a common **INTEREST**, you stay **INVOLVED** in life and reduce the chance that you will feel powerless. Being self-absorbed not only can lead to depression, but can turn you into a blinkin' bore, so to stay **INTERESTING**, stay **INVOLVED**.

IGNORE is not an 'I' word we should accept, nor is

INVISIBLE. In a 1992 *Guardian* article about television producer Julia Smith, a young staff member is quoted as saying '... she's almost the same age as my granny. So I treat her the same way I treat my granny. I ignore her.' If you feel this is happening to you, INSIST on your right to be seen and heard.

S is the letter for sadness and sickness, but we would rather it be for SINGING and SEX. SINGING can be great fun, whether done alone or with others, and it STIMULATES the respiratory system. The same can be said for SEX. If you think you are too old for the latter, consider the story of the 90-year-old woman who, when asked at what age a woman loses interest in SEX, replied, 'I don't know. You'll have to ask someone a lot older than I am.'

And as for SINGING, forget what anyone might say about your voice, crackles and all. You can always SING to babies and they will love it. SO ...

G is for GRANDPARENTING. You do not have to be a biological parent to be a GRAN. The actress Cloris Leachman once said, 'Why can't we build orphanages next to homes for the elderly? If someone's sitting in a rocker, it won't be long before a kid will be in their lap.' Maybe you could form a rent-a-lap service? Being near small children is a great tonic. Children are wonderful speakers of truth, too, if we listen to them, so use them for your reality checks. It is much easier to accept a truth from a naïve child than an adult with his or her own agenda. Children also give great hugs (see **H** below).

R covers REACHING out to others who can help you RAISE hell, RABBLE-ROUSE, RAGE against personal and social injustices and RALLY ROUND your favourite cause. Discover just how much political power a group of old people can have. Even if you are unable to get out to meetings or if your mobility is limited, you can offer to make phone calls, write letters, stuff and seal envelopes. Hold a meeting or a working tea at your own place and invite as many people as the space will hold. You will have the added benefit of company and conversation while you accomplish the task. Most important, you will be directing your **RAGE** where it belongs rather than turning it inward on yourself.

A is for **AUTONOMY**, **ACTION** and **ALLIES**. By **AUTONOMY** we do not mean the kind that says 'I must be able to do everything on my own with no help,' but what social psychologist Carol Travis describes as 'a kind of autonomy that means having the power and self-confidence to determine one's own best interest.'

As we have pointed out, identifying one's own best interest after a lifetime of being more concerned about the interests of others requires conscious effort, lots of practice and monitoring. It means being ready to re-define your interests as times change and circumstances become different. But **A** also indicates **ANTICIPATION** of what your best interests are going to be, given an **ARRAY** of possibilities. You can take **ACTION** now to assure that your best interests will be served in the future. As painful as it may seem at the moment, you will be **ASSERTING** your wishes and will be helping those who may become responsible for you.

At the very least, keep an up-to-date Will and be sure someone else knows where it is. If you have wishes about living arrangements, funeral or other ritual service, distribution of household possessions not specifically mentioned in the Will, or other opinions, put your requests in writing now so that there will be no question later of your capacity to make decisions. One person said that she went through her house and put labels on the bottoms of things, saying a bit about the origin of the piece, its monetary or sentimental value, and what disposition she wanted to make of it.

Get **ADVICE** now about taxes, estates, probate procedures and so on. The more you can **ACCOMPLISH** now, the more energy you will free up for more disgraceful pursuits. And as in all things, it helps to have **ALLIES** who can help you identify your best interests and **ACCOMPLISH** your goals.

C is for **CELEBRATE!** A good cause for **CELEBRATION** is your becoming a **CRONE**, if you remember that in mythology a **CRONE** is a wise old woman, respected and revered. Some contemporary feminists are reviving the tradition of **CELEBRATING** the power of the **CRONE**, who represents the Third Age of Woman in the Maiden, Mother-Figure, **CRONE** progression of archetypes.

If it seems right to you, gather a group of friends of any age and hold a simple ritual to mark and **CELEBRATE** your becoming a wise old woman. This need not be a religious or spiritually oriented ritual unless you want it that way. Any excuse for a **CELEBRATION** will do, and it can be held whenever you choose and as often as you like.

While we are on the letter 'C', remember that **CURIOSITY** may have killed the cat, but you are not a cat. You will never grow stale if you stay **CURIOUS** about things outside yourself, recapturing your child-like wonder.

E is for **ENGAGEMENT**. No, not necessarily as in planning to be married, although you could do that, too, if it suits you and you do not already have a spouse. By **ENGAGEMENT** we are referring to connectedness, which we keep stressing because we think it is so important.

There is a popular theory in social psychology that says that when people start getting old, they begin a process of disengagement, a cutting off from people and the world around them in anticipation of the ultimate disengagement, death. Rather than looking for the circumstances that limit or preclude ENGAGEMENT, the theory presumes that old people *want* to disconnect. In fact, given a decent standard of services, adequate care and the opportunity to maintain contacts, there is evidence that old people want to stay connected even up to and through the dying process.

F We cannot stop talking about making and nurturing good FRIENDSHIPS. FAMILY can be very supportive and helpful and we are not minimising the contributions that FAMILY members make, at least in some cases. But having FRIENDS in similar circumstances with whom you can share FEELINGS and FACE FEARS will move you FORWARD in your determination to live disgracefully to the end.

U Be UNDULY UNDIGNIFIED! You have earned the right to dress and sing and dance any way you please. You could even take up the UKELELE. So come on, UNLOCK your inhibitions.

L is for LIBERATING yourself from unnecessary LUGGAGE. LIGHTEN your LOAD by LETTING go of whatever is holding you down. Decide for yourself which possessions are the ones you really still want and then dump the rest. Otherwise it will be too LATE for you to make the decisions yourself and someone else will make them for you. If later on you must move to smaller living quarters or into a group situation, the task will be easier if you have already eliminated unnecessary ballast, and you may be surprised at what you won't even miss.

And always remember to LAUGH! Besides the therapeutic

effects of **LAUGHTER**, seeing the funny side of life helps to keep the bad parts in perspective. Libraries and bookstores carry books on the benefits of laughter with suggestions on how to find humour in situations. Try watching comedians on the telly, or go with your friends to observe the primates at the zoo, or whatever tickles your fancy. The best **LAUGHING** is the kind you do with people you **LOVE** when you can help each other find humour in what might otherwise be depressing situations. This does not mean never feeling lonely or sad or depressed. It means striking a balance so that the bad times do not begin to overwhelm you.

TRY new **THINGS** and **TRY TO** do the same **THINGS** differently. As Eleanor Roosevelt advised, 'You must do the thing you think you cannot do.' You will not need to go out looking for challenges – life will present you with plenty of them.

O has got to be **OUTRAGEOUS**. This can take many forms, depending on your inclination and willingness to call social graces into question. There are those of us (who shall remain nameless) who have used the facilities of posh private clubs and hotels by simply walking in as if we belonged. No one wants to challenge a dear little old lady, after all. Another form of **OUTRAGEOUSNESS** is to wear whatever you like without regard to what is supposed to be appropriate attire for women 'of advancing years'. Or eat pasta for breakfast and corn flakes for dinner, if it suits you. You get the idea – now it is up to you to put it into practice in your own ways.

Another way to be **OUTRAGEOUS** in old age is to **ORGANISE** political action. This can be on a local level, for instance to advocate a needed service. Stay or become active in an already **ORGANISED** group that works for something you feel passionate about. To grow old disgracefully does not mean thinking only of yourself, or that you are uninterested in what happens in the future. No matter how limited your participation, when you are involved in doing something that stirs you, you cannot feel totally powerless.

T again. This is perhaps the most important letter, because it stands for **TOUCH** and be **TOUCHED**. Old age is not a contagious disease, yet many people shy away from physical contact with ageing bodies as if it were. **TOUCHING** and being **TOUCHED** are **THERAPEUTIC** and can be done at any time without any special equipment or chemicals. **TOUCHING** does not have to have sexual connotations, although that is certainly an acceptable outcome. **TOUCHING** reminds you that you can still feel sensations and that you are not alone. This leads us to ...

H is for **HUG** and **HOLD HANDS** a lot. If you have an intimate partner, then he or she can be a primary source of **HUGS** and **HANDS**. Friends are also important sources. We highly recommend group hugs – they feel wonderful! Perhaps some ailments need to be diagnosed as the symptoms of **HUG** deprivation.

Another important H is **HAND** down your knowledge. Leave a family **HISTORY**. Tell about your experiences, the changes that have taken place in your lifetime, and **HAND** on your food recipes. See Chapter 1 for *our* stories.

E ENJOY! EMERGE! EXPRESS your positive as well as your negative feelings. And give yourself opportunities to EXPRESS EMOTIONS.

E Indulge your **ECCENTRICITIES**. Too many old people are afraid to let anyone know how they are feeling because of fear that they will not be heard or, worse, that they will be either ignored or thought a nuisance. Women especially worry about burdening others or being thought silly or undignified. Be an **EXCEPTION**!

N Say **NO** to the stereotypes and myths about old age. Let people know what you **NEED** and when you **NEED** it, and accept help. Even though it is hard to admit that we may not be able to do everything for ourselves any longer, we only limit our possibilities by being too proud to ask for help.

D Have we mentioned **DANCING?** At one Hen House session on Egyptian dancing, an 88-year-old participant who was physically limited nevertheless stood in place, tied a scarf around her hips, and swayed to the music. So **DEFY** expectations. This is your big chance to do what pleases you without worrying about being conventional. **DO** it!

And finally, **DISCUSS DEATH**. The more you talk about it, the more you take the charge out of the word. Again, this is where friends your own age are invaluable, because family members often feel they must protect you and themselves from the topic. So we end with a quote from Scottish writer and poet Muriel Spark:

> *If I had my life to live over again I should form the habit of nightly composing myself to thoughts of death. I would practise, as it were, the remembrances of death. There is no other practice which so intensifies life. Death, when it approaches, ought not to take one by surprise. It should be part of the full expectancy of life.*

We wish you a long and disgraceful very old age!

THE JOYS OF AGEING *Barbara*

When you are young the future stretches so far ahead that ageing is something that happens to other people, not to you; you feel that there will always be another chance, another time. I am sure that when I was younger I would have found the title *The Joys of Ageing* a contradiction in terms. What could be joyful about ageing? In my family we had too many examples of negative role models in the old women around us, greedy to share our lives, needy and demanding. When I thought about my old age I dreaded becoming like them.

But here I am in my sixties and it feels wonderful. I keep wondering what the flip-side will turn out to be! No aged parents to care for and worry about; no dependent children living at home; no work responsibilities since my retirement; no major health problems; enough money to get by on; loving children not too far away; grandchildren to love and cherish; interests to pursue when I have the time and inclination; and, perhaps the most important, many friends to share the good times and the bad.

The difference between my old age and that of my mother and aunts can be found in this network of friendships. On balance I think I might say that this is one of the best periods of my life, full of good times, rich friendships, love and laughter. How long can this joyous time last? We know that in the last part of our lives we have to face both our own ageing and that of our friends, and also the deaths of people we love and ultimately our own deaths too, but this knowledge makes the present pleasure all the more precious. As you grow old you need to treasure every sunset, every shared moment, in the awareness of its transience. This heightening of pleasure comes with age and it is an unexpected bonus.

Memory plays some funny tricks as you get old. Incidents from the past come to mind with every detail intact, while the title of the book you have just enjoyed reading completely escapes your mind. However, this amnesia has its advantages; when I said to a friend recently, 'Please stop me if I've already told you this story,' her reply of 'What makes you think I'd remember it!' was enormously comforting. If you can admit to your failing hearing, eyesight, breath, energy and memory with good grace and good humour, it will go some way towards defusing the irritation they might cause in others and give you some good laughs too.

What are the other joys of ageing? Well, you do not need to dress to impress, you can dress to please yourself. Instead of cooking as a chore you can share the planning, cooking and eating with friends. You can spend more time with your friends, and when the focus of your life shifts away from your family and into your networks of friendships you free yourself to be you. And then you also free your children; they can say 'We don't have to worry about Mum, she's having a great time.' The important message to learn is to love yourself, your old familiar self, and to care about your own life. At this stage in the game that takes a high priority.

For who knows what comes next? The next stage of our lives holds many frightening and unanswerable questions. What if I become ill? Will I be able to manage on my own? How long will I be able to cope? What if I become senile? Who will look after me? We all experience these fears and anxieties, they crowd into our minds in the small hours of the night. They can't be banished entirely because they are realistic fears; there are many aspects of ageing which are to be feared. But if you share these fears with friends and build networks for helping each other, as your final old age approaches you will have done the groundwork for dealing with the changes it will bring, so that you can go on living disgracefully and joyfully for as long as possible.

THE JOYS OF BEING SIXTYISH
Anne

I feel free, for the first time in my life, to live my life, my way. There is no longer anyone, real or imagined, who can prevent me from following my own path – no father or mother, no husband, no boss. And equally important, I no longer feel that I have to be nice, have to be liked by all around me.

Structure is out, spontaneity in – although I have to admit it is not easy getting the balance. If I want to go to the cinema first performance Monday afternoon, that's OK; if I want to sing as I walk on the heath or fly my kite, that's OK. I recently bought a T-shirt, pink and purple, with orange sleeves, and another with the names of 'Wild Women' printed on the front – they are amazing! Comfortable pants, comfortable shoes, comfortable shirts. If I want to scramble to pick up conkers before the little boys get them, that's OK too!

Ageing has brought me many gifts. Retirement at 60 has left me free, for the first time in my life, to follow my own desires and needs. I am enjoying the perks of free travel in London, concessionary theatre and cinema and museum tickets, no prescription charges. Little perks, but still a novelty.

I want my future to be a recapturing of the joys and delights, curiosity and enthusiasm of childhood. Playing pooh-sticks, hugging in a circle of fir-cones, lying on the fresh grass looking at the stars. These are things I enjoy doing with other women, women who like to play, women who are in touch with earthiness and goddess wisdom.

I also need time for stillness and silence – an inner, meditative, contemplative time. Time for solitude, for being alone. It feels important to be in touch with my body, to 'dialogue with the unseen parts of my body' – I believe that in this way I can dispel 'dis-ease', and go into ageing and death without terror. Crying and tears are for me a wonderful release of repressed feelings, a valuable safety-valve.

I still do not always know what I want, but when I do, I would like to think I could ask for it. Who can say what will feel important tomorrow or next week? I like the openness and lack of structure, the time and space to allow whatever comes my way.

A GOOD LOOK AT GROWING OLD
Edith

A couple of years ago I was playing a modified version of Frisbee with my younger grandson. Finally out of breath, I asked him to stop as I could no longer continue chasing the frisbee which I never managed to catch. 'I'm too old for a game like this,' I said. He refused to accept this statement. 'You're not old, you are like the young seed of a carrot,' he countered. 'Besides, Dad says you can do anything.' I never really understood his descriptive metaphor but now that I'm coming up to 75, I try to hold on to his image of me and when I manage to do this the pleasures of ageing come flowing into me. I forget the downside and wallow in other people's positive view of me.

It's not quite 'downhill all the way', plateaux appear on which the advantages of old age are manifest. Time is the big bonus now; there are no children clamouring to be fed or played with, no longer the need for constant clearing up and tidying, a minimum of job responsibilities, no need for the ego gratification provided by cooking myself to a standstill when I have visitors for a meal. It leaves me free to choose my activities, some but not all of which I share with my husband. I love spending time with my children and grandchildren but always with the knowledge that I can set limits on it without feeling too guilty. I do want to be available when emergencies arise, pleased and reassured that I am still able to cope.

Of course there are constraints both physical and financial to which we are forever adjusting. My walking pace is much faster than my husband's, so we evolved the system whereby I stride off and we arrange to meet for our first stop, then with additional stops on the way, we eventually arrive at our destination together. We can no longer indulge in far flung foreign travel, nor do we have the necessary energy for vigorous sight-seeing. Everything must be scaled down accordingly. Trips are more local and shorter but equally stimulating.

I am fully aware that although I flex my physical and mental muscles regularly, they will not remain at the same level; that along that downhill path I might suddenly find myself being transported in a wheelchair. It isn't unwillingness to face up to the inevitable deterioration. I do know it is around some corner for both my husband and myself. Death and disability are not topics we avoid, nor do we overlook the various permutations. We have arrived at certain decisions, should we be faced with irreversible conditions, which we hope we will be able to implement. A move into some sort of sheltered housing is always a possibility but since I haven't decided whether I want to be a burden to my children as yet, we will remain where we are, and I will continue to meet the challenge of growing old disgracefully.

And the trouble is, if you don't risk anything, you risk even more.
Erica Jong

RECIPES FOR A DISGRACEFUL OLD AGE

Barbara's Recipe

INGREDIENTS:
    A lot of laughter
    A few tears
    Much love
    Warm friendships
    Large amounts of fun and frolic

METHOD:

Take a group of women, well seasoned.
    Add all the above ingredients in appropriate
    quantities. Mix well, stirring with vigorous
    song and dance. Stand back!

The resulting joy, humour, delight, energy
    and chaos is guaranteed to lift your hearts.

Shirley's Recipe
Sufficient for single portion only

INGREDIENTS:

- 1 woman (fresh but cool)
- 1 sense of humour
- 1 imagination
- zest for life
- seasoning
- 1 barrel of Champagne, or, a sufficiency of mother's milk

METHOD:

If woman has been frozen, ensure she is quite defrosted.

Prepare, using all flesh, bones, heart and muscles. The latter give extra strength and flavour.

Marinate for at least 60 years in Champagne or mother's milk.

Season well but don't make it too peppery.

Sprinkle liberally with zest for life, together with the experience and humour which gives a uniquely attractive tang and appearance.

Test for tenderness. It needs to retain a certain toughness.

An added piquancy can be achieved by stuffing the woman with a favourite pickle which also helps preserve her.

Serve on a bed of friendly good wishes, luck and delicacies to suit personal taste.

NOTE:

You may be tempted to devour this exciting woman in a rush. There is no need to do so for, if well prepared, she will last quite a while.

BIRTH OF A GRANDSON, FEBRUARY 1992 *Irene*

(written on the day she became a grandmother)

The old woman danced in her kitchen
'I'm a gran, I'm a gran, I'm a gran!'
Her shoes fell off and her toes were bare
She flung her apron into the air
And all the pins fell out of her hair,
'I'm a gran, I'm a gran, I'm a gran!'

The old woman sang in her kitchen
'I'm a gran, I'm a gran, I'm a gran!'
Her voice was cracked and out of tune
But her heart was high as a runaway balloon
And the winter sun shone down like June
'I'm a gran, I'm a gran, I'm a gran!'

The neighbours came into her kitchen
They said, 'You may be a gran
But you look just like a demented hen,
It's quite disgraceful, especially when
You're over three-score years and ten!'
'Push off,' she said, 'I'm a gran!'

On the train the wheels were repeating
'You're a gran, you're a gran, you're a gran!'
It seemed like a lifetime rolling past
But breathless she reached her goal at last
And whispered as she held him fast
'I'm your gran, I'm your gran, I'm your gran!'

DISGRACEFUL TO THE *VERY* END
Edith

At the end of 1989, I resolved that the following year 1990, was to be my clearing out year. The accumulation of long unworn clothes, household paraphernalia, books and, most important, my large collection of *New Yorker* magazines, would have to go! These stacks of magazines are my link with my roots, and I have collected this weekly magazine on and off over the last 40 years.

I have had no end of viable suggestions for their disposal but equally I can counter them with endless reasons for their retention. These weeklies kept me in touch with the big and little goings on in my home town and elsewhere. Through the excellent cartoons I kept up with the changing American sense of humour and as a bonus the literary, music and art criticisms were always illuminating.

I'm proudest of the issue in August 1945 that was entirely devoted to Hiroshima and the Atomic Bomb. Everything was deleted except this long and momentous account by John Hersey on the reactions and the after effects on the people of Hiroshima of that historic, first Atomic Bomb explosion. It was in an issue of the *New Yorker* magazine that this significant gesture occurred, a magazine that occasionally was considered frivolous and elitist.

How could I desert this splendid publication that was to repeat this responsible reporting of domestic and world events in subsequent issues? Well I haven't; this Act of Cleansing never took place in 1990 nor in 1991, nor did it happen in 1992. I am now ready to accept that I don't want it all to disappear, especially my security blanket of *New Yorker* Magazines. Clutter is and always has been a way of life for me. I am not an orderly person with a logical place for each and every thing. I feel reassured that I am prepared for all emergencies with extra clothes, blankets, dishes and even reading material. I do realise I'm being very disgraceful, leaving someone else to clear up my mess, but perhaps whoever is landed with this chore will find it equally engrossing.

UNDER THE STAIRS *Barbara*

I remember a confrontation with a child over the washing of hands before sitting down to eat. Defiance from small person, words of authority from me – 'No hands washed, no tea!' Legs apart he stood firm, not wanting to lose face. 'Well, I'm not going to wash *this* finger,' holding up a grubby but triumphant small digit.

I know how he felt, as I put my house in order ready for my final old age. A recent move to a much smaller house has meant that I have had to make some ruthless decisions. I found good homes for all the surplus furniture, linen, blankets and kitchenware. I gave load after load to a worthy cause for a jumble sale, some of which I actually retrieved on the day of the sale. But there were many small things I could not bear to make decisions about, not valuable things but precious nevertheless. I found an empty tea-chest and began to fill it with these mementoes; old photographs, letters, boxes, postcards. Bit by bit it was filled to the brim.

I have not looked at this tea-chest since moving but it gives me comfort to know that it is there, in the cupboard under the stairs. It is my grimy finger, cocked in defiance at that unfair superior power which moves our lives inexorably to their end.

MEMENTOES *Barbara*

Sleep will not come easily tonight.
Thoughts of old age, helplessness, senility,
Circle a slow dance through my mind.

My thoughts drift from room to room,
Into cupboards, shelves and drawers.
What treasured memories I find.
These pebbles, round and smooth,
Warm to the touch, bring straight to mind
The smiling faces of my friends,
The soft sighs of the waves.
This matchbox, holding one fair curl of hair,
Remember which child's and why it was saved.
A file of childish writings, stories, notes
'I love my mummy.' Remember who wrote that.
Love-letters written in brown ink,
Tied with a ribbon, not re-read for years.

And when life ends will all these things
Mean anything to anyone but me?
They have their sense, their meaning
Just within my heart.
Without them I am poorer.
All the rest can go but never these.
If I were aged, blind, infirm,
I could hold a pebble in my hand,
Warm to the touch, and remember.

A LETTER TO MY CHILDREN *Barbara*

While of sound mind and more or less in full control of my faculties, there are some things I need to say to you all. I am afraid that if I don't say them now I might leave it too late, beyond the time when I will be able to make rational decisions.

I hope to retain my independence for as long as possible. This may mean that I have to pay for help, but I do not expect it from you or your partners – except for the occasional shelf or front-door lock, or minor jobs of that sort.

If I reach a point when I cannot live independently I do not expect any of you to provide me with a home. I hope and plan to make arrangements with some of my friends to live together in some sort of sheltered accommodation but, failing that, I will have to find the most acceptable place I can and if it uses all my savings – well, they are *my* savings!

If, by then, I am unable to make decisions for myself, you may have to jointly find the best place for me but none of you should feel guilty about not taking on the burden. I do not want you to do so – whatever I might be saying at the time.

I do not want my life to be prolonged artificially once the quality of life I value has gone. I hope that this will not be for many years but, ultimately, this decision may be yours to implement and I want you all to know that those are my wishes.

My belongings are just things and there is nothing of great value. When the time comes, what has not already been shared is yours to share. Please do it lovingly.

You are good loving kids and my life has been richer for having you all, through good times and bad. I have loved seeing you all grow to adulthood and watching the cycle of life as you have had your own children. I don't need to tell you what joy they bring to my life.

And, finally, my wish is to be cremated, but apart from that I leave the details to you. I believe that funerals are important rites of passage for the living, not for the dead. I hope that you will have a party and remember me with love and laughter.

PREPARING FOR DEATH *Shirley*

When my mother died I found six sets of fish knives and forks, all pristine in their felt-lined boxes. They had been wedding presents which had lain in a cupboard, largely unused, throughout the following 65 years of her life.

There were also tea-chests of 1930s books which she and my father had got as special offers from the tabloids of their day. Books like the out-dated *Home Educator*, *Home Doctor* and *Household Tips* which long ago had lost their significance with the advance of technology.

Of this musty collection the only things I valued and retained were the love letters of my once-courting parents. I had no need of the fish cutlery and the life-style it had represented, or the myriad of hoarded knick-knackery of history. But I understand the temptation to hoard when their lives were spent in the same home for the major part of their marriage.

But it was no fun for me to sort through. What an object lesson it turned out to be. I decided then and there that I would not submit my children to a similar agony. Even so, each time I have moved home I've found I've accumulated unnecessary things yet again. But, I must say, the reduction of possessions and what they symbolise has become easier since my growing-old-disgracefully friends and I have shared the recognition and reality of death. The honesty and revelations of this group have helped me face up to the challenge, without fear of what it means and signifies.

I am now more willing to clear out not only my cupboards, but also some of the jumble in my head. No, I don't want to die, but I can no longer, nor do I wish to, pretend that death is not there ahead. I'm more determined to make the most out of the *now*, keep my wits about me and, while I am still relatively sane, consider such implications and consequences as reduced income, diminished brain power, declining health and yes, dare I say it, death.

I've had a foretaste already of becoming an incoherent old lady. I think one word and another comes out. I confuse the names of people I know well. The process seems to have started and it is frightening. My friends and family trip me up with good natured humour when I malaprop my way through a story or confuse one person for another. But it hurts every time it happens, nevertheless. Will I become a laughing stock in time, looked at with condescending affection – with kindly allowance made for a batty old lady? Disintegration of my mind is more frightening to me than that of the body.

For the body has always performed better or worse according to how I feel and it seems easier to adjust to that although real disability may happen. But it is not inevitable. True, I cannot walk as fast as once I did, but that is still faster than many others and, where is the need to hurry so much anyway? As long as I can get up the stairs to my flat with a few pauses along the way, I'll cope. I don't fear death itself but gradual disintegration, pain and the ignominy of dependence.

The prospect of a limited income worries me less than the loss of health. Having been brought up in the 1930s with memories of my parents saving everything possible for recycling (even though such terminology was not then in our awareness), I have a lived experience of making do on a pittance. I have a vivid memory of my father's string box in which the tiniest fragment would be saved, and of the newspaper he would tightly wind to make firelighters. My mother would save every item of outgrown clothing to reassemble in another form, and no leftovers were ever wasted. So 'reduced circumstances' are something with which I am prepared to cope.

What preparations have I made to cope with the declining years ahead? My Will is made and the contents are known to my sons. I've written my fairly full life story and shown it to them. This provoked questions on which I was able to elaborate, unlike the many unanswered ones which have gone to the grave with my parents. I've taken what steps I can to ensure some continuing income for as long as possible. I've bequeathed my eyes and kidneys.

Many of the cobwebs in my head are being dusted down but many still remain. I have not yet addressed such vital matters as whether I want to be kept on a life support machine if my present greed for an active, vigorous life becomes an empty unreality. I've thought about the sort of music I'd like to die to and the sort of wake it might be nice to be celebrated with, but I haven't quite faced up to the challenge of sharing my plans for the funeral, nor the baked meats!

Shall I make these decisions for myself, share them now, or leave them for others to contend with? I'm sure it's more 'grown-up' not to pretend that death won't come, that decisions will have to be made. So why not discuss it now while I am still able to do so?

It's not just a matter of what flowers to put on my grave but whether I want one at all, whether I should be kept alive in intolerable circumstances if I can't express my choice at that time. The mere fact of working through these thoughts gets me a little closer to their resolution. I'm getting there but I still have some way to go.

Apart from all the practical fears of dying, the saddest

one is the loss of friends, their companionship and laughter. I will miss those who mean so much, with whom words are sometimes unnecessary. Every time one of my peers dies I get closer to my own mortality. I dread the stage of living only in the past without a worthwhile future – unable to give and only able to receive. I hope something happens to me before then.

ABOUT DEATH AND DYING *Mary*

I remember someone saying to me, 'I never think about death.' And I remember saying, 'I think about it every day.'

It's not dying I mind so much as being dead – dead for ever – and ever – and ever . . . .

I cannot bear or live with that truth, it being the one and only certainty we ever know. The only way to bear it that *I* know of (since I can't believe in life after death) is to pretend to myself that I am immortal – that the experience of *being*, of retaining the capacity for happiness will last on and on and on . . . .

But then I think of my mother's end. She died two years ago aged 93. The lessons I vowed I would learn from all the regrets and confusion of feelings that still belong to that time, come back to me.

I would like my own daughters to feel more a sense of ease about my going. And if I intend this to be so there are important things I need to attent to . . . . So far I have only *half* thought about making these preparations. (How *can* one prepare for a *final* ending, my pretending immortal soul cries out!) But to get on with the tasks . . . . There are some things that are obvious and easy – making a Will. I can tick that one off. I did that years ago. Sharing things out before I go?

Could I do that? Labelling things? Trying to be fair among four rivalrous daughters – impossible.

What I *should* do is gather them all together and tell them what I want to happen – be the matriarch. First – no quarrelling (not serious enough, anyway, to keep bitter feelings on the boil). Tell them that I have made my own arrangements for being looked after when I reach that last stage. This means I've got to find somewhere – good residential accommodation with nursing facilities attached, somewhere nearer one of them – where? Nearer to which one? Difficult . . . !

In my Will I've said my body is to go to a medical school for the use of students. I remember my third daughter, Marion, saying 'No!' to that. So at this family gathering I'm planning, we'd need to talk this over again. But I'd like to stick to my plan – why not? Every medical student must need a body of their own to work on – especially the women (my student might even get quite fond of me!)

Then all my friends and family can have a get-together to celebrate my life, re-tell the old stories. And sing a hymn – my favourite – 'The Day Thou Gavest, Lord, is Ended.' And flowers and tears and laughter.

It is the hardest part of life, is dying. (So how do other people manage it?)

I want most of all to be able to say my goodbyes. I know I need to do some more thinking about this . . . perhaps there would be no goodbyes at this family meeting. But at a time that seemed appropriate to each one. Not goodbye so much as to say what stays in the heart, yet needs to be spoken.

How would I like to be remembered? 'Honestly', is the first word that comes to mind. Family memories that have got embellished over the years are one thing, and I know there will be many of these – some with me included, some without. But when I am remembered for myself, let it be as someone *open* – open-hearted, open-minded and with open arms.

PS If I'm immortal, I have a long future ahead and I can plan for it. Fantasies – yes – fantasies. I am living in a beautiful house – a group of growing-old-disgracefully women together. If one of us can't read we read to each other. The whole place is looped up so that the deaf can hear and never get left out of any conversation they want to be part of. There is always a driver available – I don't have to drive myself anywhere I don't want to. There is laughter and comfort. It would have to be big, this lovely house, so that my sister could come too when she needed to; and it would have to be near a BR station so that I could get away and so that people with rail cards, instead of cars, could come and visit.

'Is there anything you'd like me to bring back from the village?' asked the neighbour of an old lady in the early stages of senile dementia.

'Bring me back the ends of words,' she replied.

Heard on radio programme:
Looking Forward to the Past, September 1992

ACKNOWLEDGING LIMITATIONS
Anne

'I don't want to hang up my ballet shoes yet,' said an older woman I meet early each morning, when we swim in a beautiful lake on Hampstead Heath. We were talking of the limitations brought on as we grow old. Swimming in this idyllic place, edged with willows and irises, and covered in water-lilies, is an important part of our lives. I already have one limitation – I will only swim there from June to September, when the temperature of the water is above 60° Fahrenheit.

I no longer run for buses without getting wheezy, and dread the day when I may not be able to walk or even drive. Could I be trapped at home, unable to go out on my own, unable to negotiate steps and stairs, or, worse still, totally immobile, a prisoner in a chair, dependent on others for my basic requirements?

My memory already plays tricks on me, and I fear senility. Will I become unable to make decisions for myself, or become child-like in a world of my own – making telephone calls to relatives in the middle of the night, wandering the streets without aim like a lost soul? The thought of losing control terrifies me.

Each limitation brings an ending, a little death.

I do everything I can to maintain my 'ease' and prevent disease. Meditation has become an important technique – quietly cross-legged on a cushion, back straight, observing my breathing; I feel calm and still, my heart beats more slowly, my shoulders drop, tension goes from my neck. Music also helps me relax.

I often cry – it is a great release. I keep a journal, which acts as a confidante, a vessel for containing my deepest fears and feelings of happiness and sadness.

I believe that body and mind are closely linked to provide a harmony and balance, which I hope I can maintain far into the future.

THIS WILL PASS *Barbara*

A few years ago I was seriously ill following a major operation. Life became a matter of survival, touch-and-go in a physical sense but even more, a question of finding the strength for survival in a spiritual sense. One of my friends gave me a book, *The Painter of Signs*, by R K Narayan (Penguin 1990), in which a young Indian, destitute and despairing, spends his last rupee on a message from a soothsayer. The message reads 'This will pass'. These words jumped out of the page at me. They became a kind of talisman for survival.

I did not take the message to be passivity but awareness of the cyclical nature of life. I have learnt that there are times when depression sweeps over me and I awake with leaden heaviness. At such times it is easy to feel that you will never come out of your depression, life seems grim and hopeless. But this will pass. I now allow myself time to feel the depression, even wallow in it, in the sure knowledge that it will follow the sine curve of life, it will pass and better times will return. Does this sound terribly Pollyanna-ish, finding good in everything? I only know that it has worked for me and often the upward curves, when I feel like rejoining the human race, seem all the better for the contrast with the lows.

I love the changing seasons, the dark short days of winter, the promise of spring, the warm light of summer, the colours of autumn. Each has its place in the cycle of the year and its very transience adds to its attractions. I do not think I would like to live in a tropical country with no seasonal changes. And in the same way I feel that life needs its light and shade – and both will pass.

KEEP IN TOUCH *Anne*

I read an article a few years ago that reported on a medical conference where someone presented the idea that four hugs a day acted as an antidote for depression, eight hugs contributed greatly to mental stability and twelve cuddles could promote real psychological well-being.

As we go into old age many of us are living alone, without a partner to hug and cuddle, without physical contact with others. The great popularity of cats and dogs among older people is attributed to the need for something or someone to stroke and fuss over. As small babies, unless we are very unlucky, we get all the hugs and cuddles we need. As small children, trying to separate and grow towards independence, we sometimes get them, but not always. I believe that, for the rest of our lives, we yearn and long for that intimacy and holding that was ours, without condition, as tiny babies.

I intend to keep in touch with my friends and family in a gentle, loving, physical way. A hand on the arm, an arm around the shoulders, a kiss, a hug. I value the group-hugs of my special friends, standing in a circle, arms around each other, heads close together in the centre. We then start a low chant, voices rising until the energy we create reaches a warm, vibrating climax until we lovingly part.

So I will offer hugs and cuddles, and request them from others when I need them. I cannot have too many. Anyone reading this article, please note!

I look forward to being old and wise and audacious.
Glenda Jackson

COPING WITH THE UPS AND DOWNS
Shirley

There are some Sundays when I am at home and the phone never rings. No-one knocks on my door. When I was working full-time such a day would have been a relief, a welcome break from the rushed, hectic week. Now that I am retired and have escaped from that rough and tumble it is the other way around and I miss the contact with those who themselves are still in need of that weekend respite. They have their own lives to lead.

So some Sundays are good and some are bad. I can choose to be miserable and lonely or I can look to my own resources – welcoming the silence or creating my own distractions. Where once I would mope without that call from the children or friends, I now phone them if that is my need. If there is somewhere I want to go and there is no one to go with, I'll go alone. It may not be such fun but it is better than not going at all. If I'm feeling inactive, now is the time to be self-indulgent, to read, kick off my shoes and dance, count the flowers on my balcony, make a cake or just be a lazy slob.

It's so easy to feel sorry for myself. It requires an attitude of mind to avoid that trough. But with the message TODAY IS THE FIRST DAY OF THE REST OF YOUR LIFE that I've taken on board I've decided to avoid self-pity. Life is too precious to waste. And, strange to say, since I've become more positive about my ageing, and more aware that my needs are not necessarily the same as for others, I've experienced fewer lonely weekends! Those that I have I thoroughly welcome and enjoy.

KNOWING WHEN I'M HAPPY *Mary*

So easy to write about the past, but harder to write about the future – when you're 68!

But there are lessons I have learned. The first lesson is to *know* when I am happy – to be able to say to myself, walking down the road to the paper shop in the morning, with the sun shining, 'Yes, I'm 68 – and I'm happy!' I never expected to be saying that at such an age!

But now it's good to be free of the responsibilities of children and job. I don't need to try to make my mark professionally any more. So the second lesson I have learned is to let go. I still get cards and letters and even invitations sometimes, from ex-students who have gone on to take a degree, who look back at their second chance in education for which I was responsible. And I feel a great sense of satisfaction. But I can let go too.

I'm glad I don't have to worry about sex, about getting pregnant any more. I don't need to help any more lame dogs over stiles and I don't feel I've got to go on hoping to change the world any longer (though I still support the causes I believe in – with money if not with time).

One of the best things I have learned is to be glad to be a woman – even an old woman. We've *survived* – unlike so many women of earlier generations. We don't need to feel sorry for ourselves or pushed out of sight any more. There are more of us old women – enough of us to be strong, to use our strength together, to make our own mark on the world.

But the ups and downs of old age – the stage of being disgracefully old, elderly, dependent, housebound – how would I cope with that? I have often thought that this will be the time when I re-read and relive all the holiday diaries I have kept, but never read – Cuba, Trinidad, Spain, the Soviet Union (as it was then). This will be the time to reread old letters, all the stories I've written, the poems and verses, to sort out old family photographs and treasures, the children's drawings. So many treasures I've kept over the years.

But will there be joy enough in the task, or will it be too painful to dwell on these memories, knowing that the years can never, never come again? How to keep up my spirits when they sink so very low? I know I need people, company, music, the phone. It may be mostly listening – keeping hold of the feeling of being involved in other people's daily lives, still knowing who it is they're talking about – still asking 'Did you enjoy ...?' whatever-it-was. If my sister and friends were already dead that would be the hardest thing to bear. I don't know yet how it could be borne – except to say again: *'Rage, rage against the dying of the light....'*

Thoughts such as these bring the idea of euthanasia to mind. I would like to be able to feel that I was in control – could choose the manner and the time of my own departure, hard though it is to try to imagine the circumstances. I have never believed in an 'after-life' – but some ritual, some celebration of my life, some feeling that it was a good time to go, of acceptance of my own death. This is the most I can hope for – a sense of being part of the process of the cosmos in time and space and spirit.

It helps to talk, to write down my thoughts here – to share them with other women of my own age. One thing we all agree about – is how important it is to look after your health at this stage in your life. And we exchange tips – what to eat and what not to eat mostly – mine is to eat a fresh orange and carrot every day!

And to have a laugh – to laugh! That's the thing we need most of all. And we're learning now what fun old women can have together. And every year there are more of us! So rage! Rage on! The message has to be – The more the merrier to keep the light shining.

GIGGLES GALORE *Shirley*

Giggles galore
As we fell on the floor
Having talked of our joys, of our pains.
Was it music or rhyme,
Enjoying good times
That brought us together again?

Twas the lure of our hearts
And the edge of remarks
That lingered on laughter and love
About sisters and mothers
Or fathers and brothers
What matters right here not Above.

Disgraceful our theme
We are not has-beens
But into the future we go.
Defiant we'll charge
And not be submerged
By a world that does not want to know.

Whatever may turn out
We'll meet without burnout
And live every hour of each day
We'll face all that comes
With satisfied hums
Disgraceful old women, we say.

WHAT, *US?* 'AUTHORS'? *Shirley*

We've written a book
Come see and come look
What us, you may ask
What a very big task?
At your time of life
When you're widow, or wife?
Yes we've done it at last
About future, and past.
There's life in us yet
And there's more we can get
From the sharing of friends.
We're jolly old hens.
Right through till our ends.

Till then we'll stay winning
As disgraceful old women.

A FANTASY FOR THE YEAR 2000
Anne

I am 70 today! International Women's Day, 8th March, 2000. I am having a huge celebration with all the people who have been significant throughout my life. Tomorrow I will be with my wonderful friends in the Hen Co-op, as we struggle to write *Growing Old Disgracefully* No 7, with firm hand and alert mind and undiminished inspiration!

The challenge of introducing into my life 'something new every day' is becoming more difficult – so now I am attending courses in parachuting, deep-sea fishing and horse-jumping to keep fresh and supple and active.

Tired of living in 'little boxes' in quiet desolation, I am sharing a large, rambling house, deep in the countryside, with other like-minded women. We each have a self-contained flat within the house, with views over the valley and the distant hills, but there is also a large communal kitchen and living-room. We make our own bread, jam and marmalade, and bottle fruit from the orchard. We collect and dye wool, spin it and weave it into beautiful clothes and tapestries. We write (of course), and paint and carve wood, and praise the Goddess for our bounty.

I have four grandchildren, and I love being with them. My son has returned from the Far East to buy the house he has always wanted in wildest Wales, where he has converted the stables into a studio for me, so that I can visit him and easily continue my creativity in that lovely environment.

Politicians no longer think only of themselves, but really care about the lives of the electorate. Food is shared throughout the world and no-one goes hungry. Warring factions have put down their weapons and acknowledged their love for each other, even as I have resolved all my resentments, hates and angers and acknowledge my love for others.

I am whole – a physical, emotional and spiritual being, whose mind is attuned to those other aspects of myself. My energy flows in a continuous spiral – I know myself and accept my shadow.

The Hen House is a spiritual meeting-place, for peoples of all nations, creeds and colours – with a 20-year waiting list for admission, because people are clamouring to be there. Cars are no longer used, except for emergency needs, and there is a clean, efficient form of public transport linking every part of the globe. It is quiet and unobtrusive. Fresh air has been re-introduced, and silence, except for the songs of the birds and the sound of the wind.

I pray that I may continue to live to enjoy this time.

A CELEBRATION IN THE YEAR 2000
Edith

Our writing group, all six of us, are foregathering to celebrate the launch of our latest effort, the fourth book we have written together. The three previous ones, all with the similar subject of Ageing Disgracefully, had been tremendous commercial successes. Now, here we are on the 31st of May in the year 2000, half-watching a gigantic cake covered with candles numbering our combined ages, being wheeled into the centre of the room. We are discussing anxiously how our newest venture might be received. The focus is still 'old women' but we have enlarged our area of investigation to *Old Women in Non-Western Societies: An exploration of the sexual habits of old women in these cultures*. We have chosen this outpost of civilisation, high in the Peruvian hills, to hold our celebration and the media worldwide have joined us here, ready, willing and able to relay our every word to the waiting world outside.

SPACE ODDITY *Shirley*

It's funny sitting up here on the wall. That's where I often wanted to be before I was reincarnated as a fly seven years ago, back in 1993. From up here I can look down on Barbara, Anne, Edith, Mary, Maxine and myself through time and space.

Since publication of our book in 1993 so much seems to have happened to us. I suppose that's because of the way the ideas in the book caught on with so many people from all over the country.

We've all got a bit greyer and thinner on top in the seven years but the feeling of togetherness seems to have got even stronger – if that is possible. The adrenalin which started to flow in the writing process began pumping even harder when we appeared on Wogan's resurrected show. We felt like pop stars but the audience was full of old women whose lives had been changed after reading the book. I think we disappointed Terry who had expected elderly belly dancers but we entranced them with our circle dancing which has now caught on throughout the country in evening classes, Women's Institutes, religious gatherings, political marches. 'If you sway together, you stay together,' – that's become the catch phrase that has inspired so many people, broken down barriers and infected them with goodwill towards others.

We've lived to see a film version of *Superhens*. Wendy Hiller played Barbara; Katherine Hepburn, Maxine; Maureen Lipman, Edith; Vanessa Redgrave, Anne; Maggie Smith, Mary; and Glenda Jackson, me. When they come to make *Superhens 2*, we want to play ourselves 'cos that's what the reviewers asked for. We've made a lot of money from book sales now it is in its eighteenth edition. I've extended my flat to make a permanent study to weave in. Anne has a woodcarving studio and has exhibited at various galleries. Barbara has won a prestigious prize for her maths book for young would-be Einsteins. Edith won The Most Beautiful, Vigorous, Disgraceful Great Grandmother competition, Mary has published her fourth successful novel, and Maxine has been honoured with a special award from the American Civil Liberties Union.

Talking of flying, I think they've noticed me up here on the wall. I'd got itchy and flew around a bit, perhaps getting too nosy, wanting to see them at close quarters.

They've got annoyed with me. They're looking for a fly swat and are after me. Oh dear, will I get away ...? The alarm is going. I seem to be in my own bed. It was only a dream. ... Or was it?

CHAPTER SEVEN

The Last Word . . .

It is more than three years since the six of us got together to talk about writing a book. During that time we have enjoyed many good times together, week-ends and longer holidays, staying in each other's homes, sharing cooking and chores. Our writing has given a focus to the time we spend together and, as we have concentrated on each theme, our discussions have become almost group therapy. There are things which we have written and thoughts we have shared which we may never have told anybody before. We felt safe within the group and have supported each other.

Imagine how we felt when our dream of getting the book published became a reality! Could we bear to have our intimate thoughts displayed for all to read? What about the feelings of other people we had written about? What about the revelations of our private lives? We were forced to re-read everything we had written in the light of these questions. Some details had to be expurgated, others rendered anonymous; some pieces had to be shown to relevant dear ones to get their blessing before we could commit them to print. In the end we changed very little and we have tried not to lose our honesty. The very fact of sharing our writing with the people concerned with our lives created opportunities to say things which all too often are left unsaid. We have been able to tell them how much they mean to us and what we have learned from them. We have been able to tell them that we love them and how they have enriched our lives. We have also, through talking about our writing, found it possible to discuss the difficult subjects of death and dying, to express our wishes and needs. Not surprisingly, we have all talked to our friends about the progress of this book and this has, in many cases, created opportunities for others to bring out their own deep feelings and fears.

Our lives have been changed for the better by working on this book and in this final chapter each of us has added our last words to sum up what it has meant to us and what has happened in our lives since we first met at the Hen House.

. . . from Shirley

It started with earrings. My rejuvenation and denial of an inevitable slide into decline as old age came to meet me, I mean. My mother had left me several earrings which I started to give away to friends who had the necessary pierced ears that I did not have. Fashion in morality had obviously changed between the time my mother had her ears pierced and my middle class youthfulness by which time it had become 'common'. However, my wise young friends rejected my gifts, recommending that I get my own ears pierced. I took their advice and have never looked back, advancing with leaps from my mother's marcasite to longer and longer dangles of wood, metal, ceramic, plastic and glass.

The earring was symbolic of my recovery and sense of fun. I hold happily responsible my close women friends whom I discovered on the therapeutic journey which began on a counselling course and led eventually to this group of co-writers, the Hen Co-op. These few years have been especially joyous, with no holds barred.

I thought I had been honestly open before but there is something special about old women together who have lived through similar traumas of history.

The difference here is that we have been addressing similar issues of ageing from the same platform of retirement. Through the sharing of confidences, emotions have become deeper and more profound as we have learned to trust each other more as the months have progressed. We have broken taboo subjects like facing death, loss of health and sexuality and so on which we have not been able to discuss at the same level with younger friends. Oh, the relief of sharing previously hidden apprehensions and fears and the delight of laughing with each other, having done so.

By learning about other women's tribulations and survival strengths it has been easier for me to acknowledge my own. By admitting to and sharing my weaknesses, I have discovered the others have suffered similarly, putting each into perspective. A sort of Old Ladies Anonymous group, you might say.

The constant talking about serious matters, the greater focus through addressing them in writing has been strenuous but liberating. We've ridden the storms to the end of the rainbow which contains rich friendships that will go on and on.

I've come to an inner peace and delight in living which obviously shows, despite the rapid greying of my hair. My younger friends who helped me celebrate my sixtieth birthday, left remarking that they couldn't wait to be 60! At that same birthday I had invited my son to share his thirtieth, but he refrained. Between then and now has come the exciting interval of shared writing, shared caring, shared secrets, shared dancing, shared fun – that has given me a positive anticipation of the future. I no longer hesitate to give my exact age, or lie about it but indeed say it with pride.

Maybe something of my happy acceptance of ageing

and determination to live every day to the full has now infected my reluctant son because he's now invited me to share his sixtieth birthday – when I will be 90! As he said it, his own children were sitting in their pushchair. 'I'll be the one in the pushchair then,' I remarked. But he laughingly retorted, 'You'll have to be strapped down!'

. . . from Maxine

Five years ago if anyone had tried to tell me that at the age of 60 I would meet a group of women in England, that we would become fast friends and write a book together, I would have said 'You're bonkers!' But I did and we did and it has been a life-changing experience.

Part of the metamorphosis, I must admit, came from being on a year's sabbatical leave which gave me an opportunity to step back and look at what I was doing with my life. But I could not have been as successful in making changes without the support and encouragement of my new friends.

Over the past few years I have watched myself become more assertive, more self-confident, better able to set boundaries. I no longer believe that if I don't do something myself, it will never be done or it will be done wrong. I can say 'If this is done someone else's way, it will be different from my way, but that is OK. And if it never gets done, then it must not have been so important in the first place.' I could not have felt this way three years ago.

Writing this book with five other people also pushed me into confronting my own control issues. I had to keep reminding myself that this was not *my* book but *our* book. I had to put into practice all the rhetoric I have spouted for years about the ideas of co-operation and credit-sharing. I found out that it really does work to say that each person will contribute what she can and receive according to her needs. It felt good to step out of the hierarchical mould into a decision-sharing mode.

Since we started the book I have two new grandchildren, making six in all. Looking back at how much my gran meant to me has made me realise how much I want to give love to and be a good role model for my own grandchildren.

I love England and having the opportunity to spend six months of the past year living in London and travelling around to the different parts of the country has been like a fantasy come true, made possible only by the generosity of my special friends. My life has been enriched beyond measure.

I am back at my demanding job now, trying to hold on to the growing-old-disgracefully model. I think the people I work with are in for some surprises. I look forward to retirement in a few years and who knows what the next phase will bring? I hope it brings fun, lots of hugs, quality time spent with the family and friends and many disgraceful adventures. Stay tuned!

... from Edith

After the last group meeting at our flat, my husband suggested that we ought to consider holding all our sessions here. He had enjoyed having his meals with us and had been sufficiently stimulated by the talk to refer to the project as 'our' book. In a minor key, he too was tuned into our network; inevitable considering my degree of involvement especially during this past year.

For me it has been a voyage of discovery about myself and the interaction of women working together towards a shared goal. This was sometimes painful and difficult as I was forced to come to grips with my own shortcomings. The writing never came easily to me, as it did to all the other members, and although I am more comfortable with what I write, I have come to accept my limitations.

Ultimately I have flourished in this environment, gaining confidence as the work progressed and as I learned to share my anxieties and intimacies, welcoming the support and nourishment I received. Initially it had been intimidating to be with women who were mainly ten or more years younger than I and yet were able to be so much freer and more intimate in their relationships with each other. It took me time to feel sufficiently secure within the group to be able to adopt the same open approach. But learn I did, and many are the benefits that accrue to me. Coming together regularly with members of the writing group gave me an opportunity to create a new working space and with my husband's agreement, to spend more time away from home. It provided a measure of freedom, enough to satisfy my current needs. Now, feeling less confined, it's easier for me to deal with my husband's retirement and ageing.

It is not only my husband who feels strongly connected to 'our book', it has spread to the rest of the family. This summer our group rented a cottage in Devon for a week of concentrated writing, enabling us to meet up with my son and daughter and their respective families who lived nearby. It gave my writing companions an opportunity to put a face to the people I discuss so frequently as well as giving the members of my family a chance to meet the women who have been so important to me at this period of my life.

Despite all the agonising and feelings of inadequacy that the writing project generated, I feel certain it has added an extra dimension to my life at a time when I least expected it and when all the indications are for the opposite to occur.

... from Mary

It felt cold coming back into my house yesterday. I went upstairs to find something warm to put on – a lavender-coloured jumper, hand-knitted, lacy, in very fine two-ply wool. My mother knitted it before she died. I stood for a moment thinking of her, how glad she'd be to see me putting it on. But she wouldn't have felt very sympathetic to the idea of Growing Old Disgracefully – to the idea of this book.

I feel guilty that I don't miss her more often. When she died I was holding her hand, it was a hard time for her, for all of us. Now the feeling of the preciousness of the time I have left never leaves me. But I am happy. Yes – I say to myself this is happiness – most of the time. I never expected to be as happy as this when I retired. It feels like a very surprising, risky, complacent thing to be saying.

I've just come back from a Growing Old Disgracefully Reunion at the Hen House.

'I've got used to being a serious person at home,' Elizabeth said. 'I wouldn't be silly at home like I was here last night, playing silly games, prancing about. ... That's what I need, that's what I came for.' And the others knew exactly what she meant. 'We'll get a holiday cottage and have a week together in the Spring,' they said.

Writing this book, being with so many different women at the Hen House, I realise again what a great experience it's been. No wonder I'm enjoying my retirement even though it's not likely to last!

Circumstances change, economic circumstances in particular change. Fewer and fewer women are able to afford such treats as a Growing Old Disgracefully course at the Hen House. At one reunion I've been to there were only eight of us. We discussed (briefly) the economic and political situation in Britain, the tragedies happening all over the world. We have not protested, we have not been disgraceful *enough*. There's not enough time left .... But if not women, then who will save the world? My heart aches for the old comrades who have struggled all their lives for socialist ideals and practice. But I tell myself it can't be the end of that story. There has to be hope, still.

Meanwhile – sometimes – I rejoice. There are still dahlias, soft apricot coloured, out in my garden and roses, one or two white ones, and red geraniums hanging in their pots on the wall. And there are many things to look forward to: getting on with my novel for example. I've never written a novel or any other kind of book before I became involved in this one. I've always wanted to, and now that I am retired I can make the time.

The main thing on my mind at present is the 'next stage': whether to move nearer to one of my daughters, to move to sheltered accommodation or to stay put. We often talk about it, groups of women at the Hen House, and we say, 'Couldn't we all move in together and share a spacious house and garden, each of us having a room of our own, surrounded by good friends and support when we most needed it?' Another Hen-House – for the last roosting! But where? And when? And how? It seems such a good idea.

What stops us is all the force and habit of ingrained individualism in a society like ours. But one family, one house, one old woman, surviving alone? Hanging on till the end?

What we most need is the courage to do things differently, collectively – old women coming together, a large warm, loving house with lots of room for us to grow old disgracefully in.

... from Barbara

My autobiography ended with the sentence, 'It was the need to find something more that led me to the Hen House in July 1989.' And I did indeed find something more, more than I could have hoped for! This book bears testimony to the way my life since then has changed, filled and flourished, flowered and acquired a new focus. I would not have believed that there were such rich friendships still to be made at this advanced stage in my life. Working on the book has meant that relationships between the six of us have a strength and sense of purpose beyond mere friendship. We have had a reason for meeting each week or for going on shared holidays and our times of relaxation together have felt like time well-earned.

Through the Hen House I have become part of other networks of friends who meet regularly, not just to talk but to give each other support. Some of these new friends are married or in partnerships but we come together as individuals, not as parts of couples. At the same time, I cherish my old friends and see them as often as possible. Their presence brings continuity to my life.

So, now that I have retired, far from missing the job I loved where I had worked happily for 30 years, I am finding a whole new life. Yes, there are times when I miss the comforting structure of the work routine; there are times when I have a sense of panic at the constant need to create my own life, to make things happen, but these times are becoming fewer as I learn to adapt to my new freedom.

Sometimes I experience an odd twinge of guilt, like the phantom pain in an amputated limb. I feel that I ought to be phoning or visiting my aged mother, aunt or mother-in-law – then I remind myself that over the last few years they have all died and that I don't need to feel guilty about them any more. And I do sometimes miss them, particularly when there is good family news such as the birth of a grandchild. Even my ancient cat has gone to the great cattery in the sky and, though I sometimes miss her presence, I certainly do not miss her incontinence and moulting hairs.

I read and watch the news with horror. I used to believe that there were solutions to the world's problems and that we were moving towards a better world. Now all the old certainties have gone, I no longer feel that I know any of the answers. I still feel a great anger at injustice and cruelty, but at the same time I have a sense of sad helplessness at how little we as individuals can achieve. So I send money, support protest organisations and attend rallies but out of commitment rather than hope.

I remember fondly but with incredulity the years when I went out to work, ran a big house and produced meals for six every night, with minimal help. I do miss the joy and energy of a house full of kids but I doubt very much whether I could deal with it now. I have come to enjoy the peace and tidiness of living alone; it's great to see my children as they become parents themselves, I enjoy their company and love to hear about their lives but it is delightful when they leave and peace descends once more.

I am coming to terms with my own ageing and its inevitable changes but that does not mean being defeated or depressed by it. My old age and I are good friends, we respect each other and recognise how much fun there is still waiting to be enjoyed as we move onwards, accepting the limitations and revelling in the pleasures. A year ago I moved to a small terraced house, just right for one but with a little spare bedroom for visiting friends and grandchildren. The house is very compact, easy to run and keep warm. The small sitting room has a Victorian fireplace with a gas-coal fire which

I light on cool evenings. Through the window you can see my bright, warm, welcoming room and there I am, inside my own window, and it feels good.

... from Anne

I have always loved and admired literary people and read their autobiographies, biographies and letters; relished every publication by and about The Bloomsbury Group ('All their relationships were in triangles, and they all lived in Squares'), and, of course, I pretend that I am related to Virginia Woolf!

So how did I get to be a professional author? Well, one thing is certain, I would never have got there on my own. I needed the warmth, understanding and encouragement of the other five women in our Hen Co-op, the stimulation of our discussions, the sharing of the writings, the suggestions, the approval.

Looking back with wonder, I revel in the knowledge that, age 59, I met five other women who have now become so important in my life. Women with whom I have laughed and cried, shared days and weekends together, shared holidays in the UK and abroad. Days of fun and laughter, singing and dancing, as well as writing.

When I realised that this book might really be published, and was not just an enjoyable pastime, I started getting cold feet. I altered some of the contents where they referred to others in my life. I showed my life story to my ex-husband, and discussed my contributions with my close family and friends. How will others react to this more honest and open me, who has removed a few masks and defences? I hope that when other women read this book, they will identify with some of the aspects of my life and say, 'Yes, I sometimes feel like that.'

In my life story I addressed the question 'Where do I belong?' and still find it difficult to answer, although I know first of all I need to belong to myself. At present, I feel I belong most closely to the group of women with whom this book has been written. We share a project and a similar stage in life. I love my family very dearly, and belong to them through history and familiarity – I want our lives to remain closely entwined. I also belong to a women's spirituality group, and I want to acknowledge the importance of them and my other friends old and new. I know that I belong to them all.

Typing this at my desk in my second-floor flat overlooking roof-tops and treetops, my window-boxes bright with colour, I know this is not the last word, just the beginning of the next stage. So I end, as I began, with a question: Who knows what the future will hold?

The purpose of life, after all, is to live it, to taste experience to the utmost, to reach out eagerly and without fear for newer and richer experience.

Eleanor Roosevelt

Further Reading

Non-fiction

Ageing for Beginners
Mary Stott (Penguin 1981)

The Change
Germaine Greer (Hamish Hamilton 1991)

Beyond Fear
Dorothy Rowe (Fontana 1987)

For Ourselves: Our Bodies and Sexuality – from women's
point of view
Anja Meulenbelt, Johanna's daughter
(Sheba Feminist Publishers 1981)

A Fresh Map of Life
Peter Laslett (Harvard University Press 1991)

Get the Best Out of the Rest of Your Life
Jean Shapiro (Thorsons Publishers Ltd 1990)

The Girl Within: A Radical New Approach to Female Identity
Emily Hancock (Pandora Press 1990)

How to Enjoy Your Old Age
B F Skinner and M E Vaughan (Sheldon Press 1985)

Learning from Experience:
A Woman's Guide to Getting Older without Panic
Patricia O'Brien (Sheldon Press 1991)

Look Me in the Eye: Old Women, Ageing and Ageism
Barbara Macdonald and Cynthia Rich (Women's Press 1983)

Mother to Daughter, Daughter to Mother
Tillie Olsen (Virago 1985)

Old Age
Simone de Beauvoir (Penguin 1970)

On Your Own: A Practical Guide to Independent Living
Jean Shapiro (Pandora Press 1985)

Ourselves Growing Older:
Women Ageing with Knowledge and Power
The Boston Women's Health Book Collective
(Fontana Paperbacks 1989)

Out of the Dolls House – The Story of Women in the
20th Century
Angela Holdsworth (BBC Books 1988)

The Past is Before Us: Feminism in Action since the 1960s
Sheila Rowbotham (Penguin 1990)

The Successful Self
Dorothy Rowe (Fontana+Collins 1988)

Taking it Like a Woman
Ann Oakley (Flamingo 1984)

The Unrecognised Discrimination
Ed. Evelyn McEwen (Age Concern 1990)

When You and Your Mother can't be Friends
Victoria Secunda (Cedar 1991)

Woman and Ageing
An anthology by women
(Calyx 1986)

A Woman in Your Own Right: Assertiveness and You
Anne Dickson (Quartet Books 1982)

Woman's Experience of Sex
Sheila Kitzinger (Dorling Kindersley 1983)

Resources Guide

Age Concern
Astral House, 1268 London Road, Norbury,
London SW16 4ER
081-679 8000

Alzheimer's Disease Society
158–160 Balham High Road, London SW12 9BN
081-675 6557

Arthritis Care
18 Stephenson Way, London NW1 2HD
071-916 1500

Bacup (British Association of Cancer United Patients)
Cancer Information Service
3 Bath Place, Rivington Street, London EC2A 3JR
071-613 2121.
Freeline from outside London: 0800-181199

British Association of the Hard of Hearing
7–11 Armstrong Road, London W3 7JL
081-743 1110

British Talking Book Service for the Blind
Mount Pleasant, Wembley, Middlesex HA0 1RR
081-903 6666

Cancer Relief Macmillan Fund
15–19 Britten Street, London SW3 3TZ
071-351 7811

Carers National Association
29 Chilworth Mews, London W2 3RG
071-724 7776

Choice (Family Welfare Association – matrimonial, individual and couple counselling, counselling for carers)
501–505 Kingsland Road, London E8 4AU
071-263 1181

Counsel and Care – Advice and Help for Older People
Twyman House, 16 Bonny Street, London NW1 9PG
071-485 1566

Counselling and Helpful Encouragement for The Early Retireds (CHEERS)
Unit G, Amos Castle Estate, Junction Road, Brislington, Bristol BS4 3JP
0272 724002

CRUSE (Bereavement counselling – 185 branches nationally)
Cruse House, 126 Sheen Road, Richmond, Surrey TW9 1UR
081-940 4818

Disabled Living Foundation
(National register of aids)
380–384 Harrow Road, London W9 2HU
071-289 6111

Help the Aged
16–18 St James Walk, London EC1R 0BE
071-253 0253

The Hen House – Women's holiday and study centre,
Hawerby Hall, North Thoresby, Lincolnshire DN36 5QL
0472-840278

Hospice Information Service
St Christopher's Hospice, 51–59 Laurie Park Road,
London SE26 6DZ
081-778 9252

Living Will
(for information on, contact: Terence Higgins Trust,
52–54 Grays Inn Road, London WC1X 8JU
071-831 8330

National Association of Widows
54–57 Allison Street, Digbeth, Birmingham B5 5TH
021-643 8348

Older Feminists' Network
54 Gordon Road, London N3 1EP
081-346 1900

Open University
PO Box 222, Walton Hall, Milton Keynes, MK7 6YY
0908 653449

Parkinson's Disease Society
22 Upper Woburn Place, London WC1H 0RA
071-383 3513

Pensioners Link
405–407 Holloway Road, London N7 6HJ
071-700 4070

REACH (Retired Executives Action Clearing House)
– charity which directs retired executives into
useful local causes
89 Southwark Street, London SE1 0HD
071-928 0452

Royal National Institute for Deaf People
105 Gower Street, London WC1E 6AH
071-387 8033

Saga Travel Agency for the elderly
Middleberg Square, Folkestone, Kent CT20 1BR
0800-300456

University of the Third Age (national office)
U3A, 1 Stockwell Green, London SW9 9JF
071-737 2541

Voluntary Euthanasia Society (EXIT)
13 Prince of Wales Terrace, London W8 5PG
071-937 7770

CREATING THE NETWORK

Do you want to grow old disgracefully
in company with other like-minded women?
We're establishing a national network
through which we can put you
in touch with women in your area.

*For more information please send a
stamped addressed envelope to*

Growing Old Disgracefully Network
c/o Piatkus Books
5 Windmill Street, London W1P 1HF